"Drew Strait offers important, practical guidelines for opposing Christian nationalism from a Christian framework. The metaphor of 'strange worship' is an apt description of the racist idolatry of white Christian nationalism and will be a helpful tool for Christians who want to understand and resist this toxic right-wing ideology that masquerades under the banner of 'Christianity.'"
—PAMELA COOPER-WHITE
Professor of psychology and religion, Union Theological Seminary

"On a day when the tide of Christian nationalism seems to be ever-swelling in America, Drew J. Strait gives us a clear, reasoned, and hopeful alternative to resignation and despair. *Strange Worship* offers practical and faith-centered tools for Americans to witness, fight back, and join together in a mission toward peaceful community."
—ANGELA DENKER
Author of *Red State Christians: Understanding the Voters Who Elected Donald Trump*

"With its potent blend of insight and urgency, Drew Strait holds up the un-armed, multicultural church as a lantern to reveal the shadows of Christian nationalism as a misguided and dangerous perversion of Christianity. *Strange Worship* offers the church a way forward with intergenerational, interdisciplinary, and ecumenical spaces to recharge and refocus."
—LISA SCHIRCH
Professor of the practice of technology and peacebuilding, University of Notre Dame

"Christian nationalism is one of the ideologies that perverts the Jesus-way of life. Yet followers of Jesus might not know how to respond to the Christian nationalist movement, with some being tempted to throw their hands up in surrender. As Drew Strait observes in *Strange Worship*, 'The danger for anyone challenging Christian nationalism is giving into despair and paralysis.' Thankfully, Drew Strait offers a thoughtful, well-researched, biblically informed, practical way forward. I hope that all who read *Strange Worship* will be motivated to join the subversive way of peace and love that Jesus taught."

—DENNIS R. EDWARDS
Dean, North Park Theological Seminary

"Drew Strait's hopeful, disarming, and sincere book offers a practical refutation of American Christian nationalism. Grounded in a nonviolent, Anabaptist tradition of interpretation and an incisive grasp of the message of Jesus, *Strange Worship* cuts to the heart of the politicized debates now roiling American Christianity. If you are a leader or a layperson who feels stymied in how to resist the rising tide of Christian nationalism, this is the book for you."

—MATTHEW D. TAYLOR
Author of *The Violent Take It by Force: The Christian Movement That Is Threatening Our Democracy*

Strange Worship

Strange Worship

Six Steps for Challenging Christian Nationalism

DREW J. STRAIT

Foreword by Amanda Tyler

CASCADE *Books* · Eugene, Oregon

STRANGE WORSHIP
Six Steps for Challenging Christian Nationalism

Cascade Books
An Imprint of Wipf and Stock Publishers
199 W. 8th Ave., Suite 3
Eugene, OR 97401

www.wipfandstock.com

PAPERBACK ISBN: 978-1-6667-6091-0
HARDCOVER ISBN: 978-1-6667-6092-7
EBOOK ISBN: 978-1-6667-6093-4

Cataloguing-in-Publication data:

Names: Strait, Drew J., author | Tyler, Amanda, foreword.

Title: Strange worship : six steps for challenging christian nationalism / Drew J. Strait.

Description: Eugene, OR: Cascade Books, 2024 | Includes bibliographical references and index.

Identifiers: ISBN 978-1-6667-6091-0 (paperback) | ISBN 978-1-6667-6092-7 (hardcover) | ISBN 978-1-6667-6093-4 (ebook)

Subjects: LCSH: Nationalism—Religious aspects—Christianity. | Christianity and politics—United States. | White supremacy movements—Religious aspects—Christianity.

Classification: BR515 S75 2024 (paperback) | BR515 (ebook)

VERSION NUMBER 080224

For Lucy, Bo, and Dax

Contents

Acknowledgments

Writing a book on Christian nationalism is a humbling experience; the topic is volatile and complex and no one person can possibly offer *the* path forward. In wrestling with this, I discovered one of the central arguments of this book: we need a leaderful movement to challenge white Christian nationalism. On our own we lack power but together we gain momentum. I hope and pray that this handbook can help amplify the ever-growing chorus of leaderful voices and literature challenging Christian nationalism in the United States and abroad.

Two years ago, my colleagues in the Church Leadership Center at Anabaptist Mennonite Biblical Seminary (AMBS) asked me to do two one-hour webinars on challenging Christian nationalism. I eagerly agreed, with the expectation of thirty or so attendees. When over 1,300 people signed up, the church's need for resources became personal. The six steps for challenging Christian nationalism emerged out of these webinars. I wish to thank my colleagues Melissa Troyer, Ben Parker-Sutter, Rachel Fonseca, Annette Bergstresser, Steve Norton, Jewel Gingerich-Longenecker, and Cheryl Zehr—each of whom went above and beyond to support me, including my short courses on "Resisting Christian Nationalism with the Gospel of Peace." It's a miracle to be blessed with a team of people who enthusiastically support your public voice. I'm without words to convey my gratitude.

I initially pitched the idea of this book to my friend Dr. Chris Spinks, who was a beloved editor at Wipf and Stock. From the outset, Chris's enthusiasm for this project was magnetic. Over dinner before attending the Straight White American Jesus panel on Christian nationalism, held during our annual academic meeting in Denver, CO in 2022, Chris apologized in advance that he'd been experiencing brain lapses. Two weeks later, Chris was diagnosed with brain cancer. In an early email exchange, Chris wrote: "It might be hard for me to look at your project with my editor's hat on because I am so personally interested in the topic. What you have to say about Christian nationalism is incredibly important! So, combine my personal enthusiasm with my position as an editor, and I can't think of a book I would love to work on more than this." Chris, may you rest in peace, my dear brother. Your memory and impact endure, and I hope this book is a small part of that.

The relationships forged while writing *Strange Worship* have sparked my imagination and given me a sense of solidarity with a truly global community of Christians challenging Christian nationalism. I want to thank my students in Biblical Foundations of Peace and Justice and Resisting Christian Nationalism with the Gospel of Peace in spring and fall, 2023. I also want to thank the many churches (too many to list) for courageously inviting me to preach, teach, and hold classes on Christian nationalism. I'm grateful to the following institutions for invitations to lecture or do webinars: The Sider Institute at Messiah University, Goshen College, The Nehemiah Institute, ReconciliAsian, Eastern Mennonite University, Atlantic Coast Conference of MCUSA, MennoCon, and Meserete Kristos Church Head Office in Addis Ababa. I especially want to thank my students Dirriba Sori, Endaweke Tsegaw, Israel Tesfaye and Aschalew Assefa for organizing and inviting me to speak at a three-day conference on Christian nationalism in Dire Dawa, Ethiopia. Each of these communities have profoundly shaped and expanded my thinking.

My colleagues Janna Hunter-Bowman and Lisa Schirch were generous and incredibly helpful consultants on all questions related to peace and radicalization studies. My scholarly identity has been challenged and nuanced through their influence on me. At various points, my friends and colleagues David Cramer, Leah Thomas,

Rachel Miller Jacobs, Andrew Whitehead, and student Abby Her-shberger offered helpful suggestions, resources, or feedback.

Strange Worship is structured into seven chapters, one chapter for each day of the week. This is intended to encourage finishing the book in one week since the moment is urgent. Each chapter concludes with discussion questions and the conclusion includes a call and response. This material is designed for use in congregations, small groups, or with groups of friends and neighbors.

As my editor Chris Spinks's condition deteriorated, he handed this project to Rodney Clapp. I've admired Rodney's writings for years. In fact, I had already written chapter 3 of *Strange Worship* in consultation with Rodney's exceptional book, *Naming Neoliberalism: Exposing the Spirit of Our Age*. Thank you, Rodney, for your support of this project.

I'm grateful for permission to reproduce essays I wrote in whole or in part on Christian nationalism for *Mennonite Quarterly Review,* Made for Pax, *Brethren in Christ History and Life,* and The Political Theology Network.

Finally, I want to thank Amanda Tyler for writing the foreword. Amanda has taken the lead as a tireless and visionary leader for mobilizing Christians against Christian nationalism, including her testimony at a congressional hearing on anti-democratic extremism. In that testimony, Amanda argues, "Opposition to Christian nationalism is not opposition to Christianity, and a growing number of Christians feel a religious imperative to stand against Christian nationalism." *Strange Worship* is my own way of responding to this religious imperative: to stand against Christian nationalism's distortions of the life and teachings of Jesus. I'm profoundly honored by Amanda's endorsement of this project.

I dedicate this book to my children, Lucy, Bo, and Dax. I imagine that your understanding of injustice and power worship first emerged during family movie nights watching *Star Wars.* May the immense light you bring to this world be used to overcome darkness, and don't ever forget the words of Yoda: "Fear is the path to the dark side. Fear leads to anger. Anger leads to hate. Hate leads to suffering."

Foreword

> The bottom line is that Christian nationalism cannot flourish without churches and Christian influencers' consent. To challenge consent, we have to break silence and mobilize people power to shift Christian loyalties away from strange worship toward the whole life of Jesus.[1]

CHRISTIAN NATIONALISM IS THE single biggest threat to religious freedom in the United States today. It is also an urgent threat to US democracy and the authentic witness of the Christian faith. Dr. Drew Strait, New Testament scholar and pastor theologian, has written this essential handbook for Christians who are sensing a call to dismantle Christian nationalism. It is prophetic literature, calling out a great injustice and calling in the reader to move from lament into acts of repentance and repair.

As the Lead Organizer of Christians Against Christian Nationalism, I have read, learned, spoken and written about Christian nationalism for years. Even in the bountiful and ever-expanding body of work about this topic, *Strange Worship* does something new and necessary. Strait clearly and expertly synthesizes the academic books and articles, along with public polling to help explain both what Christian nationalism is and how it came to be a destructively divisive force in US society. He also squarely addresses white Christian nationalism—the entanglement of whiteness and white supremacy into Christian assertion of power—by bringing in the

1. Strait, *Strange Worship*, 117–18.

work of theologians like Willie James Jennings. White Christians, like me and like Strait, both need to hear this and also need to call on other white Christians to do the difficult work of understanding how worshiping the idol of whiteness has pulled us away from love of God and love of neighbor. Strait does this work of calling in with humility, kindness, and a yearning for justice.

He also offers a searing and biblically-based critique of Christian nationalism as political idolatry. His exegesis, particularly of Hebrew Bible texts and the "render to Caesar" passage in the Gospel according to Matthew, invites readers into a more nuanced and complicated consideration of what it means to remain loyal to God as we are also citizens of political units.

But I would argue that the most important part of this book comes in chapter 6, when Strait urges us to get directly involved in the movement to end Christian nationalism. He rightly situates this work in congregations, places where Christians are already gathered to learn to love God by living in relationship with each other and their communities. He introduces concepts of organizing and mobilizing people power and applies them to the present danger. And then he calls congregations to work in ecumenical and interfaith coalitions toward a more liberative society that serves everyone and not just the privileged few at the expense of the many who are oppressed and marginalized. I have seen the power of this kind of faith-rooted organizing in building community with Christians Against Christian Nationalism and am convinced that this kind of on-the-ground, local organizing is what is required if we will really bring about the change that we need.

In reading this book, I can tell how much Strait not only knows about the topic, but also cares about the process and the outcome. Through his teaching about white Christian nationalism in courses, sermons and webinars around the country, he has learned a great deal about how people respond to the information and best ways to move people along a journey to reject Christian nationalism and then get more actively involved in the struggle to dismantle it. I pray that this book will be a helpful guide for you and your community as you join the growing movement rejecting

Christian nationalism in favor a world where everyone can flourish with full religious freedom.

Amanda Tyler

Chapter 1

Breaking Silence

A time comes when silence is betrayal.

—REV. DR. MARTIN LUTHER KING JR.[1]

THERE'S BEEN A LOT of talk about Christian nationalism since 2016, and for good reason. The rise of Trumpism brought fusions of Christian supremacy and white grievances out of the shadows and into the mainstream. Some politicians are now even owning the descriptor, making T-shirts that boast, "Proud Christian Nationalist." "Christian nationalism" has formally become weaponized in the culture wars over who *belongs* in the USA and who is a *real* Christian.

I train pastors and leaders to educate and nurture Christ's church. As I've addressed Christian nationalism in congregations and classrooms, the question I receive most is: "How can we effectively challenge the growing influence of Christian nationalism? We understand what it *is*, but what can we *do* about it?" This book attempts to answer this question.

Thankfully, we are not without resources to imagine what resistance might look like! The flurry of interest in Christian

1. "Time to Break Silence," April 4, 1967. I take the quote from Washington, ed., *I Have a Dream*, 136.

nationalism in the past few years has produced crucial insights into its inner workings. Recent work by sociologists and historians has unpacked how we got here and how to define what Christian nationalism is. However, questions of how to interrupt its influence nonviolently remain murky at best and wholly unsophisticated at worst.

This book, then, is an invitation. It is an invitation to break silence. Silence before theologies of oppression is a posture of compliance and consent. In breaking our silence, this book invites Christians to challenge Christian nationalism by competently and specifically naming those parts of Christian nationalism that are incompatible with the life and teachings of Jesus. It is an invitation to get vocal—*together*—and articulate why Christian nationalism is a form of "strange worship." I don't use the descriptor "strange" in the title of this book to sound provocative or for shock value. In ancient Jewish thought, the worship of another god, king, or political system was thought of as a form of "strange worship"—or what ancient Jewish rabbis called *avodah zarah*.

Christian nationalism is *avodah zarah*. It is strange worship because it is a form of political idolatry, a worldview where political power and one's ethno-racial identity become enmeshed into one's controlling narrative for making sense of the world around them. This book is an attempt to challenge misplaced loyalties, to reclaim Jesus, the kingdom of God, and the global church as the primary narrative that shapes and informs followers of Christ.

The chapters that follow show *why* Christian nationalism is a form of strange worship, in both biblical and theological perspectives, and they offer practical suggestions for *how* Christians can mobilize a transformative peacebuilding movement to disorient Christian nationalism. Together, they throw the net wide to harness the collective power of anyone who finds themselves confused and concerned by the growing influence of Christian nationalism in the United States and in other parts of the world. It is written for those of us who have experienced broken relationships with family, friends, and neighbors over Christian nationalism and those who may feel uncomfortable going home for the holidays because of their family's radicalization by right-wing media and fringe YouTube videos. It is written for my Asian, Latin American, and African students who have seen Christian nationalism's dominion theology spread through their home congregations through Western missionaries and American televangelists.

It is also written for those who have left the church because of its alignment with racist, capitalist, and ethnocentric ideologies that shroud their hate for the alien and protection of the self in Christian mantras and prooftexting. It is for my conservative neighbors who repudiate Christian nationalism and for my leftist friends. It is written for pastors experiencing angst over how to shepherd congregations in conflict over political divides, for the marginalized who have experienced real, lived harm from the policies and actions of Christian nationalists, and for anyone, especially pastors, activists, students, lay persons, and professors, who are wondering *what to do about it.*

Step one in challenging Christian nationalism is to break silence.

From Deconstruction to Reconstruction

I write with a sense of urgency. Christian nationalism presents an immediate threat to the church's public witness, to democracy, to our climate, and to human relationships.

Several recent books, essays, and op-eds by sociologists, historians, and journalists interrogate and deconstruct what Christian nationalism is and where it came from. I am profoundly grateful for this work and many of these thinkers will surface in the chapters that follow. We'd be wandering aimlessly without their efforts. While the work of *deconstruction* is crucial, I worry that we are behind the ball when it comes to defining what *reconstruction* looks like. It's one thing to *know* what we are against; it's another thing to *challenge* what we are against.

Late night parody, Tweet storms, and Facebook threads stuck in algorithmic echo chambers have not changed minds. How do we go about disrupting and minimizing Christian nationalism's influence? Is our goal to evangelize other Christians—to call Christian nationalists to repent, to change their minds about God, violence, power, race, and human difference? Or is that unrealistic? Perhaps we should focus our energy closer to home, on our own communities? Indeed, how do we socialize our congregations into a Christianity rooted in the life and teachings of Jesus, a faith that has immunity from the many phobias that fuel Christian nationalism?

I won't pretend to have my finger on the pulse of a comprehensive solution. Whatever the solution and strategy, our conversations demand multi-dimensional, intergenerational, interdisciplinary, and ecumenical spaces for discussion, prayer, discernment, and some trial and error. No one denomination, church, pastor, blogger, celebrity scholar, author, podcast, or book can *fix* the problems we face. We are in this together or we are not in it at all.

But there is one thing I am certain about: I believe the unarmed, multicultural church is a crucial actor for challenging Christian nationalism in the United States. My intention is *not* to minimize the role that other institutions, allies, democracy, and political participation can have on harm reduction and equity and inclusion in our society. Platforming the church as a context for a challenger movement may be an unpopular opinion for some. I get it—we live in a moment when Christians are best known for abuses of power, hypocrisy, and fear of strangers (rather than self-emptying, truth-telling, and unwavering love for neighbor). And so, here, my intention is also not to minimize the harm churches have caused in our communities. Christians need to own this moment—warts and all—while reclaiming the church as a survivor-centered institution that holds power worshipers of all sorts accountable.

Even with these qualifications in mind, I worry that state power has the intoxicating capacity to coopt Christians challenging Christian nationalism but in a different way. As Stanley Hauerwas writes, "Religious people on both the Right and the Left share the presumption that America is the church."[2] America is not the church. I don't make this point to "both sides," the Left and the Right, or to engage in superficial "third way" whataboutism. Rather, my intention is to reclaim local congregations as a crucial space for mobilizing "people power" against Christian nationalism.

My posture in writing this book, then, is one of hope and humility—that somehow, in some small way, this book can stimulate spaces for pastors, leaders, and congregants to share wisdom, to discuss Christian nationalism and educate others about it, to wrestle with Scripture, to pray together, to repair harm, and to (re)imagine together what a just, equitable, and Christ-centered church can be and become in a world chock-full of strange worship and theologies of oppression.

Now is not a time to sit silent or embrace moderate deference toward state power out of fear of being labeled "too political." This is the church's moment to show up. Yes, this is about democracy—but for those of us who still do theology out of and for the church, this is also about idolatry and about seeing God and neighbor rightly. That matters—a lot.

Why Strategic Nonviolence Works

In the chapters that follow, I use a word with all sorts of cultural baggage: "resistance." We'll unpack it together in chapter 5, but I want to be clear that I'm not talking about "violent resistance" or political violence of any kind. Rather, I'm referencing strategic nonviolence, which serves a vital role in God's mission of reconciliation and the church's disruption of idolatry, oppression, and sin in our world.

As Christians, strategic nonviolence has been modeled for us: it was the way of Jesus and the way of the earliest Christians. The incredible success rates of nonviolent resistance movements provide ample support for what Jesus modeled: political scientists Erica Chenoweth and Maria Stephan recently analyzed 323 violent

2. Hauerwas, *War and the American Difference*, 16.

and nonviolent resistance campaigns between 1900 and 2006 that had at least 1,000 or more participants, and what they found is stunning.[3] Nonviolent movements were twice as successful as violent ones (a 53 percent success rate compared to 25 percent). Even more compelling, the long-term consequences of nonviolent movements led toward democracy, while violent revolutions, whether failed or successful, increased the chances of civil wars or dictatorships. And would you believe that not a single nonviolent campaign had failed so long as it had the active and sustained participation from at least 3.5 percent of the population?

Imagine! *What if just 3.5 percent of Christians in the United States joined an active and sustained nonviolent resistance movement against Christian nationalism and democracy's Christian enemies?* What would be needed for success? Chenoweth and Stephan point us to three ingredients for success:

1. Broad participation by diverse groups;
2. Shifting tactics that build pressure while minimizing repression; and
3. Shifts in loyalties within key pillars of an opponent's power.

I will reflect more on what it would look like for us to achieve broad participation, shifting tactics, and shifts in loyalties in the chapters that follow but, for now, please join me in mulling over another of Chenoweth and Stephan's major observations: when participation increases, success does, too.

To challenge Christian nationalism, we need broad participation. We also need clarity on our methods and processes of resistance. Whereas nonviolent civil resistance tends to focus on toppling a dictator with critical masses of people, strategic nonviolence focuses on multiple actors and tactics that contribute to a transformative peacebuilding process. This book draws on both disciplines, but with a stronger focus on strategic nonviolence. In his book *The Politics of Nonviolent Action*, Gene Sharp catalogues

---

3. Chenoweth and Stephan, *Why Civil Resistance Works*.

198 different tactics of nonviolent intervention.[4] I will draw on some of Sharp's ideas but will add new approaches from the disciplines of biblical studies, theology, and security and peace studies.

Friends, please join me in moving beyond discussions about *objects of resistance* (deconstruction) and toward actions related to *strategies of resistance* (reconstruction) against Christian nationalism.

Changing Our Posture

To effectively challenge Christian nationalism, after breaking silence, we must get our posture right. Getting our posture right is step two for challenging Christian nationalism. For full disclosure, I've found myself cursing more than usual as I absorb the news cycle in recent years. I've even had moments where I've felt a kind of inner rage. The news cycle feels like an endless flood of history repeating itself: human intoxication with power, wealth, xenophobia, oppression, self-interest, and pseudo-peace through violent coercion.

Often, it's *white* male human intoxication and self-interest—laboring to maintain the longstanding power dynamics that have knit the United States of America together since its founding. I know I'm not alone in experiencing the catharsis of late-night parodies and Tweet storms against toxic Christianity. But does any of this move the needle toward changing minds? Or, worse than that, does it have the opposite effect of polarization? How do we harness our anger against injustice and leverage that energy for the common good?

The biblical tradition of lament affords us the proper posture of protest for challenging Christian nationalism. Lament is an act of talking back to God that empowers us to tell the truth about injustice. It provides us a space for harnessing our anger at theologies of oppression and converts it into lament, a precursor to action. After all, the word *nice* does not occur in the Bible. As Pastor

4. Sharp, *Politics of Nonviolent Action.*

Melissa Florer-Bixler writes, "When we welcome this anger's presence, rather than tamping down its energy, we find the power to create a community of resistance, and that makes forgiveness a possibility."[5] *It is okay to be angry at injustice and power worship.*

Lament is a biblical tradition, or what some call "complaint prayers," that offers a dynamic liturgical tool for addressing harm and injustice. The absence of lament in much of contemporary Christian worship is a noteworthy reminder that discipleship is too often seen as a passive relationship of "coercive obedience" with God.[6] Through lament, God offers an ancient way to talk back and complain to a listening ear about injustice, abuses of power, idolatry, exploitation, and even feelings of God's absence. Lament invites God into our pain and implores God to act *now*.

It is not an accident that the majority of Old Testament psalms are laments. Israel became *Israel* through lament: "The Israelites groaned under their slavery and cried out. Their cry for help rose up to God from their slavery. God heard their groaning, and God remembered his covenant with Abraham, Isaac, and Jacob. God looked upon the Israelites, and God took notice of them" (Exod 2:23–25). Through lament, God gives us permission to be angry and to groan and protest for God to act. As Rebekah Eklund writes, lament is a prayer of protest that imagines "a world now in which there might be less tears."[7]

Lament is also an act of worship. As Mark Charles and Soong-Chan Rah write, "Lament serves as a crucial expression of worship because it is truth telling before God."[8] As injustice and political tomfoolery consume media cycles—sometimes even in the name of Jesus Christ—I've tried (imperfectly!) to harness my anger in the form of lament. This has helped me to transfer my feelings of helplessness over to God in the form of complaint.

The psalmists give us permission to not only complain, but to *complain* to God: "Rouse yourself! Why do you sleep, O Lord?

5. Florer-Bixler, *How to Have an Enemy*, 63.

6. Brueggemann, "Costly Loss of Lament," 104.

7. Eklund, *Practicing Lament*, 70.

8. Charles and Rah, *Unsettling Truths*, 9.

Awaken, do not cast us off forever!" (Ps 44:23). Indeed, it is hard not to feel like God fell asleep at the wheel when Capitol insurrectionists worshiped and prayed to Jesus as they assaulted their way into the Capitol building on January 6, 2021. *Rouse yourself, oh God! Why do you let your holy name be used by Christian nationalists to publicly make a mockery of your faithful people?*

The logic of prayers of lament is perhaps best captured by Walter Brueggemann, who has done the most to reclaim lament as a part of the contemporary church's liturgy. Brueggemann writes that lament "makes the shrill insistence that:

1. Things are not right in the present arrangement.

2. They need not stay this way and can be changed.

3. The speaker will not accept them in this way, for the present arrangement is intolerable.

4. It is God's obligation to change things."[9]

This posture of lament not only centers on the need for justice but it also expresses humans' incapacity to affect it without God's help. In this sense, my posture in this book is one of lament and truth telling: of acknowledging that things are not right, that Christian expression in Christian nationalism is not acceptable, that things can be changed, and it is God's obligation to act. Put simply, we can't challenge Christian nationalism without God's help. I don't mean this as an invitation to holy war—I mean that we need a movement of Christians challenging Christian nationalism who are set ablaze by God's love.

What's striking about prayers of lament is that they can be addressed to God *about God* or addressed to God *about neighbor*.[10] Lament gives us permission to complain to God about God and to God about our neighbors, and to ask God to change the situation. Harnessing our anger at power worship in a posture of lament is step two for challenging Christian nationalism.

---

9. Brueggemann, "Costly Loss of Lament," 105.

10. Brueggemann, "Costly Loss of Lament," 105.

While not a prayer of lament in the strict sense, the following prayer from Walter Brueggemann's *Prayers for a Privileged People* has become a crucial prayer of recentering and protest for me in recent years. I've prayed it dozens of times with students and congregations, and I invite you to pray it with me to recenter our political loyalties:

> We name you king, Lord, sovereign.
> We trust you, except sometimes we do not.
> We take matters into our own hands.
>
> We fashion power and authority and sovereignty;
> enforced by law and bureaucracy and weapons,
> we think to make ourselves safe.
> And then learn, staggeringly,
> how insufficient is our product,
> how thin is our law,
> how ineffective is our bureaucracy,
> how impotent our weapons.
>
> We are driven back to you—your will,
> your purpose,
> your requirements:
> care for land
> care for neighbor
> care for future.
>
> We name you king, Lord, sovereign—so undemocratic!
> and in naming become aware of our status
> before you . . . loved, sent, summoned.
> We pray in the name of the loved, sent, summoned
> Jesus.[11]

A Road Map for Resistance and Recovery

If you've made it this far without throwing this book across the room, I'm guessing that you have personal stories of family

11. Brueggemann, *Prayers*, 41.

members, neighbors, congregants, or friends who have been radicalized by misinformation and fringe news sources over the past fifteen years. We are living in a moment of hyper-partisanship and polarization that has impacted all of us in some way or another.

Even while I was writing this book, a family member tried to persuade me, in my own kitchen, that the Capitol insurrectionists were good patriotic Christians and that the Proud Boys are not white supremacists. I responded strongly . . . and . . . it didn't go well. A few months ago, after I finished teaching on Christian nationalism at a church in Indiana, two physicians in their sixties approached me and said, "Many of our patients have trusted us with their family's lives for over forty years, but with COVID we watched in disbelief as they refused our counsel about vaccines in favor of online misinformation."[12] While lecturing on political idolatry in rural Pennsylvania, I stayed with a post-fundamentalist family with homeschooled kids who were scapegoated by their Christian nationalist congregation for wearing masks during the pandemic. They left that congregation and have found new life in a different congregation. More recently, a student in my class on challenging Christian nationalism shared that his brother attended the January 6 Capitol insurrection. The stories of harm go on . . .

I will be the first to confess that I've had little luck fact-checking my Christian nationalist family and friends, especially from a distance on social media. Some Christian nationalists are misinformed; others better fit the profile of brainwashed. What does recovery and sobriety mean for those addicted to the homogenous echo chamber of online hate, conspiracy, racism, and disinformation? What does repentance look like? One thing at least seems clear: recovery will only happen in those spaces that we create for telling the truth. Can the church offer an alternative space for truth-telling for those entangled in online communities of psychological manipulation? I will grapple with these questions

---

12. On the relationship between Christian nationalism and COVID-19 vaccine hesitancy, see Corcoran et al., "Christian Nationalism and COVID-19 Vaccine Hesitancy and Uptake."

in the chapters that follow with the hope that it will invite you to grapple with them, too.

I'm under no illusion that this book will be an effective tool for changing Christian nationalists' minds about God, power, LGBTQ+ persons, and racism. That's not why I'm writing this book. I'm writing to mobilize Christians to challenge Christian nationalism. This is a moment where we need to normalize *preaching to the choir; it's okay to preach to the choir.* I like how my colleague Rachel Miller Jacobs puts this: "It's like the instructions on an airplane before takeoff: in case of an emergency, make sure to put your own oxygen mask on before helping your child or a neighbor." For most of us, that may mean an internal focus on our own mental health and spiritual formation, and outreach to our families, friends, and congregations. For others, it might mean some external excursions into dialogue and relationship with Christian nationalists to create spaces for repentance in the biblical sense of the word. That is, of changing one's mind about God, power, and human difference.

In the chapters that follow, my hope is to offer a preliminary road map for resistance *and* recovery. By "preliminary" I mean an unfinished, ongoing conversation and invitation to grapple with "so what?" questions. My hope is that congregations can finish this book for me. By "resistance" I mean strategies of strategic nonviolence and formation whereby Christian communities can interrupt, and even disorient, Christian nationalism's strange worship to reduce harm. And by "recovery" I mean a holistic vision of shalom, or God's peace, for the world and all of God's creation, including for Christian nationalists who might come to see God and power in a new way.

The road map for resistance and recovery that I offer is a peacebuilding process that includes six action steps:

1. To break silence.

2. To check our posture and harness our anger at injustice in lament.

3. To define Christian nationalism and educate others so that we can name the objects of our resistance.

4. To name Christian nationalism as a form of political idolatry.

5. To preach the *whole* life of Jesus.

6. To mobilize congregations as sites to build "people power" for the common good and become spaces for recovery.

The chapters that follow will systematically unpack the six steps. Chapter 2 focuses on defining Christian nationalism. Chapter 3 explores how we got here and how empathy can be a form of resistance. Chapter 4 unpacks why Christian nationalism is a form of strange worship in biblical perspective. Chapter 5 explores what it means to teach the *whole* life of Jesus and how biblical interpretation can be a tool for strategic nonviolent resistance. Chapter 6 explores how congregations and their allies can build people power to challenge Christian nationalism. Each chapter concludes with discussion questions to help facilitate the creation of spaces to break silence, lament, and share corporate wisdom with one another. The book concludes with a call and commission for the resistance.

I remember clearly the first time I resonated with Jesus' famous charge to "go make disciples of all nations" (Matt 28:19): I was eighteen years old reading Robert Coleman's *The Masterplan of Evangelism* while camping on what's called the "Devil's Shelf" (no kidding) on the Teton Crest Trail in the Grand Teton National Park. What I could never have imagined in that moment is that, one day, I would feel led to write a book on ways to challenge Jesus' followers. In hindsight, I now recognize that the evangelical gospel that I inherited from Coleman magnified the "make disciples" part of verse 19 but minimized the "teaching them to obey everything I have commanded you" part in the rest of the passage. This book is my attempt to correct that shallow and colonizing gospel: to invite Christians to incarnate the *way of Jesus* in multicultural communities of fellowship as the great hope of peace and justice for the world.

Questions for Reflection:

1. Where have you experienced or seen Christian nationalism in your community?

2. Why are you concerned about Christian nationalism?

3. What would it look like for you and your community to "break silence"?

4. What do you most hope to learn about in this book?

5. How might lament help you during this political moment of polarization?

Chapter 2

What Is White Christian Nationalism?

The subtler threat of Christian nationalism is a kind of ubiquity that leads to invisibility. For so many white Christians, Christian nationalism isn't Christian nationalism. Rather, it's just Christianity. People don't even see it and that's the deadliest threat.

—JEMAR TISBY[1]

THE THIRD STEP FOR challenging Christian nationalism is to define it. Defining Christian nationalism is important because it is impossible to resist something unless we can name the objects of our resistance. As Kimberlé Crenshaw suggests, "Where there's no name for a problem, you can't see a problem, and when you can't see a problem, you pretty much can't solve it."[2] Defining the problem—that's what this chapter is about.

In publicly naming the problem, we create the possibility for making visible those parts of Christian nationalism that are strange worship. For so many Christians, Christian nationalism isn't a deviation from the life of Jesus. Rather, *it's just Christianity*. But for

1. See Tisby, "Engaging White Christian Nationalism."
2. Crenshaw, "Urgency of Intersectionality."

Christians against Christian nationalism and those who have left the church, Christian nationalism has *taken over* Christianity.

Thankfully, we are not without good resources for defining Christian nationalism. The sheer volume of op-eds and academic studies on Christian nationalism are hard to keep up with, including for the professor who is paid to read books! While I will hat-tip this important work in this chapter, my purpose is not to offer a fresh historical analysis—that would be outside my wheelhouse anyway. Rather, my aim is to offer pastors and congregants a panoramic of Christian nationalism that will empower them to name and make its problematic parts and worldview visible to the watching world. For those wanting a deeper dive, pay careful attention to the footnotes in this chapter.

While the words that follow in this chapter may seem pointed and assertive, my goal is not to parody Christian nationalists. My goal, rather, is to tell the truth. Christian nationalists, though mistaken in their theology and worldview, are an object of God's love and desire. I want to be clear about this at the outset, and I will say more about the role of empathy in the next chapter.

So, what is Christian nationalism?

Telling a Story Beyond Trumpism

To understand Christian nationalism, we need to tell a story that goes beyond Trumpism and the January 6 insurrection. For me—and maybe for you, too—that means going back to my roots.

I was baptized as an infant in the Roman Catholic Church in Spokane, Washington. I spent most waking summer days at a family cabin in North Idaho that my grandfather purchased in the early 1960s, where "God and country" culture and the Confederate flag were regular accoutrements on the walls of taverns, trucks, boats, and T-shirts. After my mom decided she couldn't convert to my dad's Catholic faith, my parents decided to raise my sisters and me in the United Methodist Church. The Methodist Church gave me a powerful awareness of who God is and how to pray, but it wasn't until a Young Life camp in seventh grade that I became a zealous follower of Jesus. That camp also baptized me—metaphorically speaking—into white American evangelicalism.

For the next ten years of my life, I went all-in with my personal relationship with Jesus. This meant evangelizing friends at school by inviting them to Young Life club. It meant doing a deep dive into purity culture as a teenager and reading Joshua Harris's now retracted *I Kissed Dating Goodbye*. It meant reading the highly problematic *The Prayer of Jabez* in early college and praying for "God to increase my territory" as an emissary of the gospel. It meant listening to Christian ska, punk, and hardcore bands—some of which I still enjoy to this day. It meant serving as a reference for one of my youth leaders to be inducted into the secret evangelical society known as "The Family." It meant attending a Franklin Graham revival and answering an altar call when the "Power Team" came to town.

I look back and shake my head at some of this with no small amount of discomfort, especially the part that reduced the gospel to me and Jesus, or what Dallas Willard calls "the Gospel of sin management." But I also recognize that it wasn't all bad. Evangelicalism taught me how to share about my life openly with other close friends and that the life of Jesus matters. I'm grateful for that.

It wasn't until I was a college student at Whitworth University that I came face-to-face with the violent underbelly of Christian nationalism. Like every American, I will never forget waking up to the horrific terror attacks on September 11, 2001. To this day I mourn the loss of innocent life and pray for God to comfort the hundreds of families who lost loved ones on that dark day.

As a zealous evangelical Christian doing all the right things, majoring in theology and leading youth ministry, our so-called "Christian" nation's response to the terror attacks consumed me. The consensus among my family and friends, and embraced from many local church pulpits, was that violent retaliation needed to follow, and that the destruction it brought would be an act of patriotism. I was even told by one prominent New Testament professor that violent retaliation against Afghanistan and Iraq would open a way for the gospel to reach the Muslim world. Really? Where, *exactly,* did Jesus' Great Commission call us to drop bombs on innocent strangers as a missional strategy?

In solidarity with such sentiment, people waved American flags from bridges in support of the US military and drivers honked in support. Churches offered prayers for soldiers. Donald Rumsfeld, an architect of America's preemptive invasion of Iraq, placarded Bible verses on secret classified briefings while a Michigan-based defense contractor inscribed rifle scopes with biblical verses like 2 Corinthians 4:6: "For it is the God who said, 'Let light shine out of darkness,' who has shone in our hearts to give the light of the knowledge of the glory of God in the face of Jesus Christ."[3] God, apparently, was on America's side of the rifle scope as it sought to spread coercive light through violence in the Muslim world under the banner of imposed democracy.

Then, on March 20, 2003, America lit the skies with its military might to crush the Saddam Hussein regime in Iraq through its "shock and awe" campaign. Even thousands of miles away, the shock and awe felt real as news anchors strapped on military gear to ride in tanks and film the spectacle. As the night wore on, I watched from the house of my youth leader, who led me to Christ in seventh grade. To my disbelief, my beloved leader and closest Christian friends cheered, even yelped, with glee as the Iraqi night sky lit up with balls of fire, sparks, and smoke, signaling the death of strangers beneath the rubble. At the time, I was a good Reformed evangelical and came armed with "just war theory" as I made my case against the war until the wee hours of the night to no avail. Alas, my friends' and mentor's faith were anchored deep in American military exceptionalism.

The celebrated spectacle led to the mutilation of over 200,000 innocent civilians, including entire Chaldean Christian communities.[4] Christian nationalism—in its soft and hard cultural versions—is deadly.

---

3. On Rumsfeld, see Frank, "Donald Rumsfeld's Bible Verses." On the rifle scopes, see: "U.S. Military Weapons Inscribed with Secret 'Jesus' Bible Codes."

4. See https://www.iraqbodycount.org/.

Two Dominant Expressions of God in America

My experience watching the shock and awe campaign in my youth leader's living room is something I come back to often in my research as a New Testament professor. It sparked a life-changing pursuit for understanding Christianity with a more questioning posture toward the nationalist identity that had clouded my previous understanding of Scripture and, at times, suppressed my embrace of the teachings of Jesus.

As I lived into my new-found Christian identity, I started to observe that there are two dominant expressions of Christianity in the United States. The first is what some call "moral therapeutic deism" and it sounds something like this: "There is a god who created the world, looks down on us from heaven with a smile, wants to bless us, wants us to be good to ourselves and kind to others, is there for us when we are in a jam, and promises us a place in heaven if we are good."[5] Sound familiar?

The second dominant expression of God in America I observed is "Christian nationalism" and it sounds like this: "There is a god who created the world, looks down on America with a big smile, has blessed us more than any other nation, thinks our values are his values, wants to expand our influence around the world, wants us to be good to our friends but helps us defeat our enemies, and expects us to love our country as a way of loving God."[6] Sound familiar? The thing about moral therapeutic deism and Christian nationalism in the American context is that they have a porous boundary between one another. Christian nationalism and Hobby-Lobby-trinket-god-superstition go hand in hand.

In addition to telling a story beyond Trumpism, it is important to acknowledge that Christian nationalism is not unique to the United States. I'm thinking here of Russian Orthodox priests

---

5. Quote used with permission from Dr. Michael J. Gorman's blog that is no longer active.

6. Quote used with permission from Dr. Michael J. Gorman's blog that is no longer active.

who support Vladimir Putin's genocidal invasion of Ukraine.[7] I'm thinking of evangelical churches in Brazil that supported Jair Bolsonaro's authoritarian rise to power (and recent January 6-style insurrection).[8] I'm thinking also of evangelical churches in Ethiopia that are supporting Abiy Ahmed's genocidal war against Tigray in exchange for power.[9]

Christian complicity in nationalist loyalties that lead to violence is a global problem. While Christian nationalism is not unique to the United States, its expression in the United States has some distinctive features rooted in what Andrew Seidel calls "the founding myth."[10] Understanding a thing or two about the founding myth is crucial for understanding the popularity of Christian nationalism and power worship in the United States.

The Founding Myth and Christian Dominionism

The Pew Research Center recently came out with new polling data that illustrates just how deep Christian nationalism is seared into the American conscience: 45 percent of Americans think the USA should be a "Christian nation" and 60 percent of US adults believe America's founders intended the US to be a "Christian nation."[11] These numbers are stunning.

Even more recently, the Public Religion Research Institute (PRRI) asked respondents to agree or disagree with the following stand-alone question: "God intended America to be a new promised land where European Christians could create a society that could be an example to the rest of the world."[12] While most Americans disagree with the statement (67 percent disagree), the

7. See Fagan, "How the Russian Orthodox Church is Helping Drive Putin's War in Ukraine."

8. See Ellsworth and Cardoso, "Bolsonaro Shores Up Evangelical Support in Tight Brazil Election."

9. See DeCort, "Christian Nationalism Is Tearing Ethiopia Apart."

10. Seidel, *Founding Myth*.

11. See Smith et al., "Views of the U.S."

12. See "Christian Nation?"

numbers change dramatically among adherents and sympathizers of Christian nationalism (83 percent of adherents and 67 percent of sympathizers agree with the statement). Among "white" respondents, these numbers go up even more among adherents (to 87 percent) and among sympathizers (to 70 percent).

At the core of these polling numbers is what Philip Gorski and Samuel Perry call a "deep story" that goes something like this: The US was founded by white Christian men, it has a special covenant relationship with God, and is thereby specially blessed and serves a special purpose in salvation history. In the more conservative versions of this founding myth lies a theological conviction that Christians are entitled and chosen by God to rule—to hold dominion over society (Gen 1:28; Matt 28:18–19). Theologians call this Christian dominionism, or dominion theology.

Forms of Christian dominionism first emerged in the twentieth century through R. J. Rushdoony's Christian reconstructionism, but it really took off in the 1970s through evangelical leaders like Francis Schaefer, Loren Cunningham (the founder of Youth with a Mission), and Bill Bright (the founder of Campus Crusade for Christ). In separate divine visions in 1975, Cunningham and Bright claim to have received a vision of seven spheres over which Christians are to influence and hold dominion to turn the world around for Jesus. These spheres are family, religion, education, media, entertainment, business, and government.[13]

Bright and Cunningham's seven spheres of dominion went global through missionaries and charismatic leaders. It wasn't until the year 2000, however, that their ideas took on a much more *imperial* tone, when a Pentecostal businessman turned pastor, motivational speaker, apostle, and meme theologian named Lance Wallnau met with Loren Cunningham. Wallnau claims his life was transformed by Cunningham's vision of seven spheres. Instead of seeing Cunningham's visions as spheres of influence, he saw them as high mountains to be subdued for Christ. Wallnau writes, "These mountains are crowned with high places that modern-day

13. For a helpful overview of dominionism, see https://www.christiancentury.org/article/features/quiet-rise-christian-dominionism.

kings occupy as ideological strongholds . . . we do not need more conversions to shift a culture. . . . We need more disciples in the right places, the high places."[14]

Wallnau's vision led to the now widely popular "seven mountain mandate," a theological vision of politics by coercion that legitimates much of Christian nationalism's power worship in the US and other countries. Notably, Wallnau, along with what Matthew Taylor calls a "charismatic spiritual oligarchy" of leaders like Che Ahn and Dutch Sheets, were key architects for spreading conspiracies about a stolen election during the events leading up to the January 6 Capitol insurrection.[15] To date, these leaders have not been held accountable as a formal part of the Select Committee's investigation into the Capitol insurrection.

More recently, a younger generation of Christian influencers are offering more sophisticated intellectual justification for the founding myth and Christian dominionism. Andrew Torba and Andrew Isker recently published *Christian Nationalism: A Biblical Guide to Taking Dominion and Discipling Nations*. Torba and Isker founded Gab.com, which they describe as a "digital Noah's Ark to escape the tyrannical flood of censorship from the Silicon Valley elite . . ."[16] They argue that America is a Christian nation but "somewhere along the way our tolerance for evil allowed subversive agents of Satan to invade every facet of our country and culture." The idea that the US is under the control of demonic forces is a common refrain among Christian nationalists. To exorcize America's demonic influencers, Torba and Isker argue that "The time for being a Christian wimp is over. Now is the time for a masculine, patriarchic, crusader, 'Jesus is King' Christian revival."[17]

Such machismo Christian revivals are happening all over the US at the grassroots level. For example, the disgraced US general Michael Flynn has organized dozens of "Reawaken America"

14. See https://www.straightwhiteamericanjesus.com/episodes/the-new-apostolic-reformation-series-intro/.

15. See Taylor, "Charismatic Revival Fury, Ep2."

16. Torba and Isker, *Christian Nationalism*, 32.

17. Torba and Isker, *Christian Nationalism*, 34.

rallies, where dominionist leaders are calling for an "army for God" to fight against liberals' woke agenda, performing baptisms, selling trinkets, and telling a dangerous message that so-called American greatness is in decline and it is up to Christians to take the country back for God.[18] While Reawaken America may seem fringe, it is the tip of the iceberg of the most underreported and fastest growing Christian movement in the United States, called the New Apostolic Reformation (or, NAR). NAR is a loose collection of charismatic churches where dominion theology is growing at alarming rates, and a cabal of prophets and apostles are aligning themselves with right-wing politicians to take dominion over demonic spheres of purported spiritual influence as they anticipate a third great awakening and/or the return of Jesus.[19]

The desire to take dominion for God has little to do with piety and biblical values. Rather, as Michelle Goldberg wrote ahead of her time in 2006, "the ultimate goal of Christian nationalist leaders isn't fairness. It's dominion. The movement is built on a theology that asserts the Christian right to rule. That doesn't mean that nonbelievers will be forced to convert. They'll just have to learn their place."[20] Goldberg's point is not hard to illustrate. Take, for example, the congressional testimony by the Capitol police officer Daniel Hodges, who was crushed in a door by January 6 insurrectionists. Hodges testified that:

> The sea of people was punctuated by people with flags . . . It was clear the terrorists perceived themselves to be Christians. I saw the Christian flag directly to my front. Another read "Jesus is my Savior, Trump is my president." Another, Jesus is King. One flag read "Don't Give up the Ship." Another had crossed rifles beneath a skull emblazoned with the American flag. To my perpetual

18. See Hagen, "ReAwaken America Tour Unites Conservative Christians and Conspiracy Theorists."

19. I encourage readers who are unfamiliar with NAR to listen to Matthew Taylor's "Charismatic Revival Fury" audio documentary on the Straight White American Jesus podcast: https://www.straightwhiteamericanjesus.com/episodes/the-new-apostolic-reformation-series-intro/.

20. Goldberg, *Kingdom Coming*, 7.

confusion I saw the thin blue line flag, a symbol of support for law enforcement, more than once being carried
by the terrorists as they ignored our commands and con-
tinued to assault us.[21]

Hodges' testimony offers a disturbing window into how dominion
theology can mean "right to rule" through violent coercion. When
the "right to rule" is encroached on by outsiders—for example, by
non-Christians, persons of color, and LGBTQ+ persons, and so on
so forth—Christian nationalists can turn to violent means to "save
America" or "make America great again."

Christian dominionism's claim that America is a Christian
nation has significant historical problems that we need to talk
about more. In 1983, the preeminent evangelical historians Mark
Noll, Nathan O. Hatch, and George M. Marsden set out to "search"
for Christian America in a co-authored book. Their conclusion offers an even-handed and stunning rebuke of those who consider
America a "Christian nation." The authors write that "a careful
study of the facts of history shows that early America does not
deserve to be considered uniquely, distinctly or even predomi-
nately Christian, if we mean by the word 'Christian' a state of society reflecting the ideals represented in Scripture."[22] They go on to
write that the very "idea of a 'Christian nation' is a very ambiguous
concept which is usually harmful to effective Christian action in
society," concluding that, "America is not a Christian country, nor
will it ever be one."[23]

Beyond the founding myth's historical problems also lie biblical problems. According to the New Testament, there is no such
thing as a "Christian nation." The only Christian nation in the
world is what the New Testament calls the *ekklesia* (or, "church")
and it is multicultural, borderless, weaponless, and the primary
context for bearing witness to the gospel of Jesus Christ. Understanding Christian dominionism's "founding myth" can help us
tell a more nuanced deep story that challenges strange worship.

21. For full testimony, see González, "D.C. Officer."
22. Noll et al., *Search for Christian America*, 17.
23. Noll et al., *Search for Christian America*, 17, 102.

Toward a Definition of Christian Nationalism

There are several proverbial expressions among Christian nationalists that have been commercialized on T-shirts, bumper stickers, yard signs, and flags. One that I've seen around town lately feels especially descriptive and venomous. It includes a large image of an American soldier kneeling before the flag and a gun with the following message:

> THIS IS AMERICA!
> We eat meat.
> We say the pledge.
> We love guns.
> We hate terrorists.
> We stand for the flag.
> We kneel for the fallen.
> If you don't like that. Leave.

The message is clear: assimilate to "our" worldview or leave. Anyone even superficially aware of America's culture wars can read between the lines: this proverb repudiates the Black Lives Matter movement, gun reform, Muslims, "woke" vegans, and any public influencer who kneels during the national anthem. In the word "leave" we arrive at the crux of Christian nationalism's threat to our democratic values of government of the people, by the people, and for the people, whose civil rights and freedoms are protected by law.[24] Robert P. Jones, the president of PRRI, suggests that these "incompatible perceptions of America—as a pluralistic democracy or as a promised land for European Christians—are at the heart of America's political polarization . . . a vocal and engaged minority has hijacked one of our major religious traditions and one of our political parties, determined to hold the country hostage to a mythical past."[25] At the national and municipal level, Christian nationalism is holding American democracy hostage in exchange for

---

24. For a helpful overview and definition of democracy in the face of its Christian enemies, see Gushee, *Defending Democracy*, 7–25.

25. See Jones, "Virtual Roundtable."

power and privilege. This is why it is so important to understand and define Christian nationalism.

Since 2020, our understanding of Christian nationalism has come into much sharper focus through the pioneering work of sociologists Andrew Whitehead and Samuel Perry. In their co-authored book *Taking America Back for God: Christian Nationalism in the United States*, Whitehead and Perry offer the first data-driven, scientific analysis of what Christian nationalism is, based on data from the Baylor Religion Survey, in-depth interviews, and participant observation at large events. [26] In other words, this book does not contain the latest musings on what a scholar *thinks* is happening; rather, it comprises a scientific, real-time analysis of *what* Americans believe in this moment.

Whitehead and Perry define Christian nationalism as "a cultural framework—a collection of myths, traditions, symbols, narratives, and value systems—that idealizes and advocates a fusion of Christianity with American civic life."[27] Key to their definition is the idea that "the 'Christianity' of Christian nationalism represents something more than religion . . . it includes assumptions of nativism, White supremacy, patriarchy, and heteronormativity, along with divine sanction for authoritarian control and militarism. It is as ethnic and political as it is religious."[28] The last sentence in Whitehead and Perry's definition is key: for Christian nationalists, one's ethno-racial identity becomes enmeshed with one's partisan political loyalties and religious identity. Put another way, to be a true American one must be *Christian* and assimilate to the values of conservative white Republicans.

In addition to definitional clarity, a major contribution of Whitehead and Perry's study for Christians challenging Christian nationalism is their observation that there are four postures toward Christian nationalism among Americans: rejecters, resisters,

---

26. Whitehead and Perry, *Taking America Back for God.* For a fuller review of Whitehead and Perry's book that I wrote for pastors and leaders, see Strait, "Let's Talk About Christian Nationalism."

27. Whitehead and Perry, *Taking America Back for God,* 10.

28. Whitehead and Perry, *Taking America Back for God,* 10.

accommodators, and ambassadors. This spectrum, now used widely among journalists and scholars (but recently changed to adherents, sympathizers, skeptics, and rejecters by PRRI), provides an incredibly helpful reminder that Christian nationalists are not a homogenous group, nor are those who oppose it. It's a messy world we live in. These four postures from Whitehead and Perry's study can be summarized as follows:

Rejecters make up 21.5 percent of Americans and comprise those individuals who are most educated and resistant to implementing Christian values in American public life. One-third of rejecters associate with a Christian religious tradition and tend to be wealthier and to populate urban centers, the Northeast, or West regions of the country.

Resisters make up 26.6 percent of Americans and share key demographics with rejecters, except for being slightly less educated. Resisters are more religious than rejecters (80 percent believe in a higher power, compared to only 40 percent of rejecters). While resisters are suspicious of the declaration that America is a Christian nation, they might be comfortable with the presence of religious symbols in public places. It is notable that resisters and rejecters make up almost half of the US population.

Accommodators make up 32.1 percent of Americans and lean toward Christian nationalism while holding some ambivalence toward it. Accommodators are older, include more women than rejecters/resisters, are more religious (a third are evangelical Protestant and a third identify as Catholic), and, like resisters, tend to be political moderates (47 percent identify as such).

Ambassadors make up 19.8 percent of Americans and are the least educated and oldest of the four groups (average age is fifty-four, whereas the average age of rejecters is forty-three). For ambassadors, the founding fathers were Christians and America's prosperity hinges on obedience to God's law in the Bible (but with strong preference for Old Testament texts). Notably, only 16 percent of ambassadors reside in cities—a reminder that to challenge ambassadors we need to create more relational ties between urban and rural and across class lines.

Key predictors of ambassadors include identification with political conservatism, belief in the Bible as the literal word of God, belief that America is on the brink of moral decay, belief that God requires the faithful to wage war for good, and belief in the rapture (even though the word "rapture" does not occur in the Bible). While ambassadors comprise the smallest group, they have an outsized amount of power due to gerrymandering and the ways congressional representation works in the United States (for example, Wyoming has two senators with a population of ~578,803 people; California, on the other hand, has two senators with a population of 39.24 million people).

A major thesis of Whitehead and Perry's book (and a surprising one for me) is that religious commitment is not always a vector for Christian nationalism. In fact, Christian nationalism "often influences Americans' opinions and behaviors in the *exact opposite direction* than traditional religious commitment does" on its own.[29] The relationship between Christian nationalism and religious commitment is animated by survey questions that clarify the moral priorities of each group.

Statistically significant predictors for religious practice include caring for the sick and needy, economic justice, and consuming fewer goods. For Christian nationalists, these moral priorities are either statistically insignificant or negatively associated. Of equal interest, Christian nationalists see military service as a vital component of "being a good person." Religious practice, on the other hand, tends to cultivate a negative association with military service.[30] Provocatively, while ambassadors are far more likely to condemn divorce, they are also more likely to participate in it: their marital status shows the *highest rate of divorce* when compared to rejecters, resisters, and accommodators (Fig. 4.1). This point again highlights how Christian nationalists' ethics are about political power and a particular social hierarchy—not religious piety in the strict sense.

---

29. Whitehead and Perry, *Taking America Back for God*, 20.

30. Whitehead and Perry, *Taking America Back for God*, 14.

While religious commitment and Christian nationalism on their own operate differently, there is overlap in the Venn diagram—most Americans who embrace Christian nationalism are quite religious. Adherents of Christian nationalism are "twice as likely as Americans overall to report attending religious services at least a few times a month (54% vs. 28%)."[31] This is a disturbing reminder that many churches in the US remain incubators for Christian nationalism. As Chrissy Stroup suggests, "Christian nationalists are by and large churchgoing believers . . . The only way to fight Christian nationalism effectively is to recognize it as an authentically Christian phenomenon."[32] This a call to public lament; it is also a call for Christians challenging Christian nationalism to own this moment by naming Christian nationalism as an authentically Christian phenomenon.

I want to close this section with a word of caution. The word *evangelical* has become a catch-all buzz word for painting broad brush strokes about toxic Christianity. The word could be used to classify the values of some Mormons as well as Catholics or Protestants. A much stronger predictor for the rise of Trumpism, anti-black sentiments, xenophobia, resistance to racial justice and the repudiation of women in politics is Christian nationalism. My point is that evangelicals and evangelical-adjacent persons are not a homogenous group of people, and Christian nationalist values trickle down and pervade many denominations.

I have personally experienced this in the Mennonite Church USA, which is a historic peace church. After my exit from evangelicalism after the Iraq war, I stumbled into a Mennonite congregation that was doing intentional community together in Chicago. I learned about this church from Ron Sider's book, *Rich Christians in An Age of Hunger*. In 2009 I attended the Mennonite National Convention in Columbus, Ohio, as a delegate for my church. When I sat down with a group of pastors and delegates, I shared my story with the assumption that all Mennonites are anti-war Christians and care about peace. I was stunned to learn from rural

31. See "Christian Nation?"

32. See Stroop, "Christian Nationalism is Authentically Christian."

Mennonite pastors at my table that many of their congregants had been impacted by talk radio influencers like Rush Limbaugh. Some of their congregants, in fact, had started buying guns! This experience reminded me that no denomination has immunity from Christian nationalism. Immunity must be intentionally nurtured—everywhere, including in historic peace churches.

What Is White Christian Nationalism in Theological Perspective?

Whitehead and Perry offer a sophisticated definition of Christian nationalism in sociological perspective. In theological perspective, I think Christian nationalism is best summarized as *a movement where one's God-given theological imagination is hijacked by political power.* To my short definition we can add three longer points about identity, context, and ethics.

First, on identity. Christian nationalism is a worldview where one's ethno-racial "American" identity hijacks our baptismal identity "in Christ." In other words, being white and/or American becomes a more important identity marker than our corporate and global identity in Christ as children created in God's image.

Second, on context. Christian nationalism is a worldview that sees the militarized kingdoms of this world (rather than the unarmed, multicultural church) as the primary context for bearing witness to Jesus and the kingdom of God. In other words, partisan loyalties and political power become the primary context for Christian mission and witness.

Third, on ethics. Christian nationalism is a perversion of Jesus' way of peace because it endorses state violence, police brutality, torture, and personal armament as expressions of faithful discipleship. In other words, it turns a blind eye to Jesus' example and teaching on nonviolent resistance, neighborly love, and peacemaking, along with the unanimous witness of the New Testament that the way of Jesus is a way of peace, including Paul's conversion from a violent extremist to a peacemaker.

Together, these are all symptoms of strange worship and a diseased theological imagination that has been hijacked by political power. In chapter 4, I explore what gestures and postures toward political power lead to strange worship. For now, it's important to recognize that the worship of political power has a compounding effect when done in the assembly of others. It is a kind of contagion or pandemic that multiplies exponentially among its worshipers, resulting in the production of what the apostle Paul calls "Sin" in society.

Sin, for Paul, is not merely a list of vices and peccadillos. It is, rather, a personified force that enslaves humans and entangles them in systems of injustice and cultural violence. One way to signify this is to capitalize Sin when Paul talks about it. Paul, in fact, suggests that "all, both Jews and Greeks, are under the power of Sin" (Rom 3:9), leading to societies where the feet of idolaters "are swift to shed blood" and "the way of peace they have not known" (Rom 3:15, 17). For Paul, idolatry and human-on-human violence go together. And, for Paul, the only solution to the problem of idolaters' violence is the revelation of God's righteousness, or what I translate as God's "justiceness," revealed in Christ (Rom 1:16).

In the same way that the cosmic power of Sin enslaves humans, it also gives permission—even incentives!—to its hosts to lord power over others. Some scholars call Sin a "superorganism" that encroaches on its hosts to stimulate a feedback loop that results in human hierarchies of power.[33] It is not hard to see how such a cosmic, systemic, and biblical understandings of Sin as a superorganism can help us understand what Jemar Tisby calls the "permission structure" of Christian nationalism.

Tisby writes that Christian nationalism is "an ethnocultural ideology that uses Christian symbolism to create a permission structure for the acquisition of political power and social control."[34] This permission structure has more to do with Sin than the life and teachings of Jesus. Followers of Jesus are tasked with a mission

---

33. See Croasmun, *Emergence of Sin.*
34. See Tisby, "Virtual Roundtable."

of interrupting Sin, not enabling its patterns of harm to human beings through control and mastery.

To summarize, we can define Christian nationalism in theological perspective as a worldview where one's God-given theological imagination is coopted and hijacked by political power. This hijacking leads to strange worship. Christian nationalism is also a theology of "distraction." It distracts us from our corporate complicity in Sin and participation in the life of God. It exchanges the love of God and neighbor for an "us" vs. "them" tribalism that gives permission to control others through coercion. It also exchanges God's embrace of all of humanity through creation and the cross for a narrow and fear-based vision of "my way" or "leave." Fueling this xenophobic and racist worldview in the US is whiteness—a term that demands our full and undivided attention.

Why "White" Christian Nationalism?

Since Whitehead and Perry wrote *Taking America Back for God*, scholars and pundits have debated about whether we should talk about Christian nationalism or "white" Christian nationalism. Admittedly, this is a confusing nuance since there are fringe "Blacks for Trump" groups, along with Latinos who voted for Trump because of shared Christian nationalist values.

Debates around adding the descriptor "white" have, in my opinion, been laid to rest by a recent book by Philip Gorski and Samuel Perry, who argue that whiteness is the center of gravity for Christian nationalists because data on key issues behave differently among whites than with persons of color. The authors argue that "the subtext of Whiteness in the language of 'Christian nation' and 'Christian values' becomes obvious when we see how differently our Christian nationalism measures work for Whites than for Black Americans."[35] For example, they observe that "adherence to Christian nationalism has little if any correlation with their views about racial discrimination, American religious history,

---

35. Gorski and Perry, *Flag and the Cross*, 44.

COVID-19 issues, or views on the economy."[36] Gorski and Perry's findings are important as we aim to get more definitional clarity on the objects of our resistance. The whiteness in white Christian nationalism is the epicenter of this conflict.

The best definition of whiteness that I'm aware of comes from theologian Willie James Jennings, who argues that "Whiteness is a way of imagining oneself as the central facilitating reality of the world . . . and Whiteness is having the power to realize and sustain that imagination."[37] What's disturbing is that when the power and privilege of whiteness is threatened by outsiders, violence becomes a viable option for white Christian nationalists to maintain power as the "central facilitating reality of the world."

To be sure, Gorski and Perry find that "The more that White Americans seek to institutionalize 'Christian values' or the nation's Christian identity, the more strongly they support gun-toting good guys taking on (real or imagined) gun-toting bad guys, the more frequent use of the death penalty, any-means-necessary policing, and even torture as an interrogation technique."[38] Herein lies one of white Christian nationalism's most dizzying perversions of early Christianity: It has transformed the nonviolent, enemy and neighbor loving, crucified Jesus into a violent white-Rambo-like god who pacifies human difference through coercion to maintain white power and privilege over marginalized persons.

The cultural violence of Christian nationalism remains an ongoing threat to democracy and human security. In fact, 40 percent of Christian nationalism adherents agree that "Because things have gotten so far off track, true American patriots may have to resort to violence in order to save our country."[39] In 2021, 15 percent of all Americans agreed with this statement. Disturbingly, this number has gone up to 23 percent in 2023—a reminder that threats of domestic extremism are increasing in the US.[40]

36. Gorski and Perry, *Flag and the Cross*, 44.

37. Jennings, "To Be a Christian Intellectual."

38. Gorski and Perry, *Flag and the Cross*, 96.

39. See "Christian Nation?"

40. See "Threats to American Democracy."

The fear of losing power that fuels whiteness is not difficult to stoke. One conspiracy theory that has stoked the fires of white power movements across Europe and the United States is called "replacement theory."[41] Replacement theory finds its roots in twentieth-century French nationalism but found its modern expression in French author Renaud Camus's 2011 book, titled *Le Grand Remplacement* (or *The Great Replacement*). As Muslim refugees fled to Europe from Syria's genocidal war, Camus's book stoked the fear that non-white communities are replacing white communities, a fear compounded by the idea that white birth rates are in decline.

Camus's ideas quickly jumped the pond to North American pundits, who popularized the idea on major media outlets like Fox News. Among white power extremists in the United States, talk of "white genocide" took hold in soft and hard versions. A recent poll by PRRI found that 32 percent of Americans affirm the statement that "Immigrants are invading our country and replacing our cultural and ethnic backgrounds."[42] Among adherents of Christian nationalism, this number goes up to 71 percent and among sympathizers to 57 percent (strikingly, among whites polled the numbers go up to 81 percent among adherents and 66 percent among sympathizers).

Notably, white supremacists in the United States appeal to replacement theory in their sacred fourteen words: "We must secure the existence of our people and a future for white children." Not surprisingly, white nationalists in 2017 at the "Unite the Right" rally in Charlottesville chanted: "The Jews will not replace us!"[43] More recently, in August of 2019, a white twenty-one-year-old, "proud God-loving Christian" (according to his Twitter bio), murdered twenty-three people in a Texas Walmart in an act of anti-Latino terrorism. In a manifesto posted on 8chan, the shooter

41. On replacement theory, see the National Immigration Forum's "The 'Great Replacement' Theory, Explained."

42. See "Christian Nation?"

43. On the fourteen words and other hate symbols at the Unite the Right rally in Charlottesville, see "Deconstructing the Symbols and Slogans."

wrote that "This attack is a response to the Hispanic invasion of Texas. They are the instigators, not me. I am simply defending my country from cultural and ethnic replacement brought on by an invasion."[44] The fear of whites being replaced by persons of color is a viral conspiracy theory that is deadly and inhumane. Its cruelty was recently felt as Texas troopers were instructed to push migrant children back into the Rio Grande River to deny them entrance into the United States.[45]

What is especially disturbing about replacement theory is that one doesn't have to be an ambassador of Christian nationalism or a member of the white power movement to be taken hold of by its ideas. I can think of professing Christians in my own network who have bought into the fear of being replaced by immigrants. This is one reason that Donald Trump was so effective at stoking his base. Take, for example, this Tweet from October 29, 2018: "Many Gang Members and some very bad people are mixed into the Caravan heading to our Southern Border. Please go back, you will not be admitted into the United States unless you go through the legal process. This is an invasion of our Country and our Military is waiting for you!"[46] For those consuming a daily media diet of soft and hard versions of replacement theory, the message of caravans stoked fears of replacement—indeed, only a tough "law and order" strong man can preserve and protect whiteness.

The influence of whiteness in our body politic is also reflected in recent data that suggests that economic anxiety (or pocketbook voting) had little to do with supporting Trump in the 2016 election. Rather, racial identity and status threat drove Trump supporters. As Diana Mutz writes in an article from the *Proceedings of the National Academy of Sciences*, "White Americans' declining numerical dominance in the United States together with the rising status of African Americans and American insecurity about whether the United States is still the dominant global economic superpower combined to prompt a classic defensive reaction among members

44. See Villagran, "Walmart Shooter."
45. See Wermund, "Texas Troopers Told to Push Children."
46. See Choi, "Trump."

of dominant groups."[47] Replacement theory, not economic anxiety, propelled Trump to power.

In a country where there are more guns than people, the relationship between whiteness, direct violence, and white Christian nationalism presents an immediate threat to public safety in the United States.[48] It also presents an immediate threat to the church's integrity, public witness, and loyalty to the life and teachings of Jesus. One way to challenge whiteness is to break our silence and publicly name whiteness as the epicenter of our conflict with Christian nationalism.

Why is White Christian Nationalism a Problem?

One could belabor this question with a list of problems white Christian nationalism presents to democracy and the church. But I don't want to muddle the point I want to make in this chapter: *White Christian nationalism is a problem because it distorts and perverts the way of Jesus and thereby the church's public witness.*

White Christian nationalism exchanges right worship, which is Jesus worship, for strange worship. It exchanges our *identity* in Christ for a weaponized *identity* in whiteness draped in partisan loyalties. It exchanges God's mission in the *context* of the unarmed, global church for an imperial mission in the *context* of the militarized kingdoms of this world. It perverts the ethics of the kingdom of God, exchanging Jesus' model of neighborly love and boundary crossing for fortification, segregation, and walls to protect and maintain the power and economic wealth of whiteness. It exchanges Jesus' way of peacemaking for politics by coercion.

The third step for challenging white Christian nationalism is to define it. Before discussing step four, it's worth pausing to

---

47. See Mutz, "Status Threat."

48. Experts suggest that around 352 million guns are in circulation in the United States, based on ATF data. See Mascia and Brownlee, "How Many Guns are Circulating in the U.S.?" On the rise and acceptance of political violence in the United States, see Kleinfeld, "Rise in Political Violence in the United States."

ask: How did we get here? In asking this question, I'm inviting us to explore how empathy and curiosity have potential to become a distinctively Christian strategy for countering violent extremism.

Questions for Reflection

1. What is one "aha" moment you had from this chapter?

2. In one or two sentences, how would you define Christian nationalism?

3. Do you find Whitehead and Perry's spectrum of ambassador, accommodator, resister, and rejecter helpful? If you feel comfortable sharing, where do you see yourself on this spectrum?

4. Why is it important to talk about "white" Christian nationalism?

5. Why do you think replacement theory has gone viral in the United States?

Chapter 3

How Did We Get Here?

The metamorphosis of Jesus Christ from a humble servant of the abject poor to a symbol that stands for gun rights, prosperity theology, anti-science, limited government (that neglects the destitute) and fierce nationalism is truly the strangest transformation in human history.

—RAINN WILSON[1]

IN A VIRAL TWEET, the actor Rainn Wilson (best known as Dwight Schrute from *The Office*) struck a nerve. The transformation of the enemy-loving, crucified Christ into a *white American Christian nationalist* is not only *strange*, but an audacious act of historical revision.

Adding to the strangeness of this moment is the reality that those of us who affirm the social teachings of Jesus (e.g., love of neighbors and enemies, inclusive table-fellowship, divestment of money, care for poor) are called "libtards," "snowflakes," or "socialists" for believing that the teachings of Jesus are meant to be lived out in this world. But if you affirm the values of Christian nationalism—militarism, xenophobia, meritocracy—you are considered

1. Rainn Wilson, Twitter, August 3, 2019.

a good, Bible-believing Christian. A serious imitation of Christ requires us to flip this script—and we can do so by following the example Jesus set.

Thankfully, we have good resources for understanding the historical pressures that metamorphosed Jesus from a humble servant to a militant white nationalist in the United States! I'm thinking especially of Kristin Kobes Du Mez's widely acclaimed, *Jesus and John Wayne: How White Evangelicals Corrupted a Faith and Fractured a Nation*. Du Mez offers a mesmerizing history of evangelicalism's "militant masculinity" and power worship that created the conditions where "evangelicals did not cast their vote [for Trump] despite their beliefs, but because of them."[2] Readers looking to understand this history should start here.

An overview of the rise and influence of the religious right in the US is beyond the scope of this chapter but one reflection is worth pausing for. The religious right did not emerge from a pure desire to make America look more like Jesus. Rather, as Sarah Posner writes, "The Christian right movement was born out of grievance against civil rights gains for blacks, and a backlash against the government's efforts to ensure those gains could endure."[3] It was a movement inspired by desire to maintain whites' cultural dominance.

Evangelicals' reactionary quest for power resulted in a pervasive infrastructure for leveraging power over society. This infrastructure includes, but is hardly limited to, Rush Limbaugh-style talk radio, televangelism, a Fox News media empire, personality-cult-megachurches in almost every major city in America, James Dobson's Focus on the Family, Bill Gothard's homeschool movement, the God and guns ideology of the NRA, evangelicals' allegiance to Republican lawmakers in exchange for power, and Charlie Kirk's Turning Point USA. Together, these institutions and their allies are the Trumpocene—a space where the Bible, white grievances, and the theological justification for lording power over others have converged into a durable social, political, and

2. Du Mez, *Jesus and John Wayne*, 3.

3. Posner, *Unholy*, 124.

theological movement that has reached the highest levels of the US government. While evangelicals only make up 14 percent of US society, they've built a platform for leveraging power at all levels of society, including a stacked supreme court. Indeed, with one Tweet it is now possible for a president of the United States to activate legions of soldiers for God over a mere conspiracy.

I want to hit the pause button on offering concrete strategies for challenging white Christian nationalism. During this pause, I invite you to think about the moment in which we are living from a satellite's view—to gaze down at the conditions that have created the climate for radicalization and the metamorphosis of Jesus into a white American Christian nationalist. I hope to invite you into a space of curiosity, albeit a *subversive* curiosity that opens possibilities for empathic resistance. By "empathic resistance," I'm talking about empathy + resistance. More on this below.

From #PizzaGate to #QAnon

We need to have some hard conversations about the impact of social media on human relationships and our congregations if we are to understand this historical moment. I've watched in disbelief over the past decade as people in my own social network have been taken hold of by misinformation and conspiracy theories over the idea that America is under attack by a "woke mob." Basic facts we could agree on even ten years ago—like the value of science and public health efforts—no longer feel like common ground.

The surreal power that social media has to distort reality descended on an unsuspecting pizzeria called Comet Ping Pong in Washington, D.C. during the months leading up to the 2016 election. Unbeknownst to its owner, right-wing disinformation pundits pushed conspiracies on Twitter and Reddit that Satan-worshiping liberals, including Hillary Clinton, abused children in the basement of Comet Ping Pong. The unfounded conspiracy was known as #PizzaGate. For James Alefantis, the owner of Comet Ping Pong, the ordeal became highly personal as images of his own children eating in his pizzeria were taken from his social media accounts and circulated across online platforms as evidence of pedophilia.

As social media companies looked the other way, a twenty-eight-year-old named Edgar Madison Welch drove up from North Carolina with a loaded AR-15 and unloaded a barrage of bullets into a basement door of Comet Ping Pong in search of a pedophilia ring as customers, including children, fled for their lives. Welch is now serving a four-year prison sentence but the trauma from the ordeal endures. In the words of Alefantis, "My employees are traumatized, literally have PTSD, traumatized, waiters in their twenties. I know specific people who are going to therapists, or, you know, afraid to go places because of the actions of these people. So, these are real consequences. As the federal judge said, in the case against the gunman, it's a miracle no one was killed."[4]

The bizarre #PizzaGate scandal is interpreted by many as a forerunner to the success of the QAnon conspiracy movement. Roughly one in five Americans believe in the QAnon conspiracy theory. Let me say that again: *one in five Americans believe in the QAnon conspiracy theory.* That's a remarkable figure. What emerged in 2017 as a fringe conspiracy has now been mainstreamed by the election of QAnon-adjacent politicians and highly public activists like the horn-studded "QAnon Shaman" who prayed on the senate floor during the January 6 Capitol insurrection. Recently, the QAnon supporter and US congresswoman Marjorie Taylor Greene was interviewed on CBS's *60 Minutes*, thus normalizing her brazen push of extremist views at the highest levels of government. After Greene's interview, Franklin Graham further normalized Greene's leadership for his Christian nationalist supporters by Tweeting that "I was watching @60Minutes Sunday night . . . I learned a lot. I don't know her, but I think she brings some practical, common sense to politics. You might want to take a minute to check it out. It will be interesting to see how God uses her."[5] Notably, Greene believes that the Sandy Hook shooting was a hoax, where twenty

---

4. See Hayden, "'There's Nothing You Can Do.'"

5. Franklin Graham, Twitter, April 4, 2023.

of the twenty-six people murdered were children between the ages of six and seven.

At the heart of the QAnon movement is the belief that the US government and major media outlets are led by a network of Satan-worshiping pedophiles and that there is a coming "storm" that will dismantle their power over government and media. The eye of this storm, according to Robert P. Jones, is "a common belief that there is a pervasive cultural threat to their vision of America as a white Christian nation."[6] Eighty-one percent of QAnon believers, in fact, believe that "America is in danger of losing its culture and identity."[7] For many, this storm was confronted messianically by Donald Trump himself through innuendo and coded Tweets for those with eyes to see and ears to hear. This is why it was not uncommon to see "Trump is our Savior" signs at his rallies.

According to the National Consortium for the Study of Terrorism and Responses to Terrorism (START), QAnon followers have committed 101 ideologically motivated crimes in the United States as of September 22, 2021.[8] Sixty-one of these crimes were committed by Capitol insurrectionists. On a pastoral note, it's worth noting that 41 percent of the forty-four QAnon offenders who committed violent crimes before and after the January 6 insurrection radicalized after experiencing trauma, including PTSD from military service, sexualized or physical violence, or the premature death of loved ones. Moreover, 60 percent of the forty-four QAnon offenders have documented mental health concerns. This is a reminder of how important mental health care is for preventing radicalization and violent extremism.

The power and virality of conspiracies are not new in human history. For example, after the Roman emperor Nero's death in 68 CE a conspiracy went viral that Nero was going to come back to life. The book of Revelation in the New Testament, in fact, riffs on this conspiracy to portray the anti-Christ as *Nero redivivus*—or

6. See "Persistence of QAnon."

7. See "Persistence of QAnon."

8. See "START, National Consortium for the Study of Terrorism and Responses to Terrorism."

Nero come back to life (Rev 13:3, 18; 17:8). What's new is the ability to exponentially amplify conspiracies on social media without consequences. For white Christian nationalists who believe their God-given right to rule over the US is under threat, conspiracies offer a dynamic tool to mobilize mass outrage and resistance. As Bradley Onishi writes, when Christian nationalists "feel their influence and power dwindling, conspiracies become a tool for reasserting their worldview as legitimate."[9] While conspiracies like #PizzaGate and QAnon seem patently outlandish, a conglomerate of media venues immerse Americans in "alternative facts" and take advantage of the human brains' susceptibility to misinformation and outrage.

Why Our Brains Love Fake News

We are living in unprecedented times. The social experiment that is social media is barely two decades old. We are only beginning to understand how social media impacts democracies, communities, and congregations around the world.

Facebook's mission statement boasts about "giving people the power to build community and bring the world closer together." Twitter (now, X), on the other hand, claims that "our company is built on community. Together, we can be a force for good." Such techno-optimism is good for business, but evidence is shifting the scales toward techno-pessimism as social media platforms are used for authoritarian surveillance, disinformation, polarization, and violent extremism in democracies around the world.[10]

Research shows that misinformation spreads six times faster than true information on the internet.[11] During the 2016 election, the top twenty fake news articles on Facebook generated more

---

9. Onishi, *Preparing for War,* 157.

10. Schirch, *Social Media Impacts,* 3.

11. See Vosoughi et al., "Spread of True and False News Online."

clicks than the top twenty real articles from every major publication combined.[12]

According to psychologists, fake news is an intoxicating way to distort the truth because it reinforces a human tendency to accept information that affirms our beliefs.[13] Psychologists call this "confirmation bias." Fake news, especially when paired with "information overload" or "data saturation" (that is, high volumes of articles with thousands of likes), is excellent at leveraging confirmation bias because it can cause the brain to process information with the emotion center of the brain rather than those involved in reasoning or logic.

Some studies have even shown that such emotional processing, satisfied by re-Tweets and shares, sparks a dopamine rush in the brain like a drug, creating a positive feedback loop between sharing fake news and heightened pleasure. According to other researchers, this cycle of disinformation is exacerbated by political polarization.

One group of psychologists recently analyzed the behavioral sharing patterns of 500,000 news story headlines among 2,300 Americans on Twitter and found that the inclination to share fake news had less to do with being misinformed or uneducated and more to do with hating one's political opponent.[14] In other words, hate trumps truth and fuels the spread of fake news about one's ideological opponents.

Surveillance Capitalism and Brain Hacking

Fueling the proliferation of misinformation is what scholars call "surveillance capitalism." Lisa Schirch, who is a scholar of violent extremism, writes that surveillance capitalism "harvests private data and experiences and then sells access to this data. This economic model monetizes private experiences based on tracking

12. See "Why Do Our Brains Love Fake News?"
13. See Braucher, "Fake News."
14. See Osmundsen et al., "Partisan Polarization."

or surveilling their every click on the internet."[15] This economic model incentivizes "brain hacking" by creating "an economic motivation for designing social media platforms to be addicting."[16] In other words, there is a cause-and-effect relationship between outrage, addiction, and making more money for tech-oligarchs and their bureaucrats.

Cognitive biases and brain hacking have also contributed to the proliferation of what scholars call "segregated information ecosystems." Within these information silos, Americans live in different realities about current events, which lends to declining trust, growing resentment between partisan groups, and an "us" vs. "them" mentality.[17] The ensuing hyper-partisanship, according to one recent report by leading scholars, is "undermining Americans' ability to come together across lines of differences to devise solutions to common problems. From a stalemated Congress, to local school boards embroiled in conflict, to families and friends torn apart, these dynamics touch every part of our lives and threaten the very core of our democracy."[18]

The threat to democracy is real—so, too, is the threat to the church's witness. I wonder: can congregations become spaces for dialogue and trust building to challenge brain hacking and reduce "meta-perceptions"? (Meta-perceptions are our notions of what others think about us, which can stimulate perception gaps that lead to cultural and even direct violence.)[19]

One step toward challenging polarization is to (1) name surveillance capitalism as a medium for (not against) division and polarization; (2) create spaces for educating congregants, neighbors, and family members about how to detect misinformation; and (3) to name and understand the structural inequalities that

---

15. Schirch, *Social Media Impacts*, 13.

16. Schirch, *Social Media Impacts*, 13.

17. Dehrone et al., "Renewing American Democracy," 13.

18. See Dehrone et al., "Renewing American Democracy," 13.

19. On perception gaps, see Dehrone et al., "Renewing American Democracy," 29.

have contributed to the radicalization of members of our families and communities.[20]

Third Order Suffering

In addition to exploring social media's contributions to polarization, we need to have some hard conversations about structural inequalities in our society. One of the most profound books I've read in the past decade is by Bruce Rogers-Vaughn, titled, *Caring for Souls in a Neoliberal Age.*[21] Rogers-Vaughn is a psychotherapist and pastor-theologian who is concerned about how the governing economic philosophy of our time called "neoliberalism" has impacted our souls. Neoliberalism, in short, is a mutation of capitalism from an economic theory to a moral philosophy that redefines human existence around consumption and competition abetted by deregulation and the privatization of public services (e.g., medical care, banking, insurance, social media, etc.).[22]

The result, according to Rogers-Vaughn, has been a disaster for human souls as we are forced to compete with our neighbors in a rigged gig economy of income inequality. According to this moral philosophy and purported meritocracy, those who find themselves failing in the hustle culture of the neoliberal order simply haven't worked hard enough. As Adam Kotsko argues:

> We have to be in a constant state of high alert, always "hustling" for opportunities and connections, always planning for every contingency (including the inherently unpredictable vagaries of health and longevity). This . . . requires us to fritter away our life with worry and paperwork and supplication, "pitching" ourselves over and over again, building our "personal brand"—all for ever-lowering wages or a smattering of piece-work,

20. For more suggestions, see pages 22–34 of Dehrone et al., "Renewing American Democracy."

21. Rogers-Vaughn, *Caring for Souls in a Neoliberal Age.*

22. For a short introduction to neoliberalism, see Leary, "What is Neoliberalism?"

which barely covers increasingly exorbitant rent, much less student loan payments.[23]

Kotsko tips his hand to the soul shattering forces of hustle culture, along with the entrepreneurial self where one individualizes and promotes a personal brand to leverage "success" in a hierarchical rat race. These economic and social pressures are not benign or always lucrative. Rather, according to Rogers-Vaughn, they have produced new forms of suffering wherein sufferers have no idea *why* they are suffering at all. I call this "zombie suffering."

Rogers-Vaughn discusses three orders of human suffering. The first two orders of suffering are familiar: it is the human conditions of death, grief, separation, illness, natural disaster, and physical pain.[24] The second order is human-on-human evil: war, robbery, sexualized violence, murder, etc.[25]

What Rogers-Vaughn calls "third order suffering" is sneakier, wherein the neoliberal order has created a society of depression, anxiety, addiction, intense shame, loneliness, and a sense of personal failure. He writes that, "The people I now see tend to manifest a far more diffuse or fragmented sense of self, are frequently more overwhelmed, experience powerful forms of anxiety and depression too vague to be named, display less self-awareness, have often loosened or dropped affiliations with conventional human collectives, and are increasingly haunted by shame rooted in a nebulous sense of personal failure."[26] The decline of human collectives in the United States inspired the US Surgeon General to recently publish a seventy-page report called, "Our Epidemic of Loneliness and Isolation." The data in the report is jarring, including their finding that lacking "social connection can increase the risk for premature death as much as smoking up to 15 cigarettes a day."[27] Among Americans, researchers found time spent with friends declined

---

23. Quoted in Clapp, *Naming Neoliberalism*, 51. Original quote is in Kotsko, *Neoliberalism's Demons*, 95, 119.

24. Rogers-Vaughn, *Caring for Souls in a Neoliberal Age*, 126.

25. Rogers-Vaughn, *Caring for Souls in a Neoliberal Age*, 126.

26. Rogers-Vaughn, *Caring for Souls in a Neoliberal Age*, 2.

27. See "Our Epidemic of Loneliness and Isolation."

twenty hours a month between 2003 and 2020, and time spent alone increased by twenty-four hours a month in that period. They conclude that Americans are sick, angry, and alone.

Taken together, third order suffering and surveillance capitalism have created conditions that are ripe for radicalization.

Loneliness and Online Radicalization

An organization called Moonshot CVE (Countering Violent Extremism) focuses on the adverse impact of isolation on online radicalization. Moonshot's vision is to "reach people at risk from online harms and offer them an alternative path."[28] Moonshot CVE has developed an algorithm called the "redirect method" that uses "targeted advertising to connect people searching online for harmful content with constructive alternative messages."[29] The redirect method functions as a strategy of counter-radicalization by redirecting far right audiences to testimonies from former neo-Nazis and mental health resources.[30]

In January of 2017, Moonshot CVE employed the redirect method on Google and Twitter to see if users searching to join violent far-right groups were more likely to click on mental health ads than comparison groups. They found that users looking to join these extremist groups were 115 percent more likely to click on mental health ads.[31] They also found that, during COVID lockdowns, searches for extremist content in Canada's six largest cities went up by double digits, signaling the connection between isolation and radicalization.[32]

Moonshot CVE's work says a lot about the relationship between loneliness, isolation, dwindling human collectives, and online radicalization. The famous philosopher Hannah Arendt

28. See https://moonshotteam.com/. I'm indebted to Lisa Schirch for teaching me about Moonshot's work.
29. See Moonshot, "Redirect Method."
30. See Pasternack, "One Secret Weapon against Extremism."
31. See Moonshot, "Mental Health and Violent Extremism."
32. See Moonshot, "Impact of COVID-19 on Canadian Search Traffic."

observed an interconnection between these dynamics when she wrote extensively about totalitarianism in the aftermath of World War II. In her monumental *The Origins of Totalitarianism,* first published in 1951, Arendt argued that totalitarian regimes exploited isolation and terror toward ideological ends. She writes, "What prepares men [and women] for totalitarian domination in the non-totalitarian world is the fact that loneliness, once a borderline experience usually suffered in certain marginal social conditions like old age, has become an everyday experience."[33]

One way to challenge Christian nationalism is to make loneliness a smaller part of humans' everyday experience. The church is uniquely positioned for this work as a network of relationships and friendships, not a building. In naming our pandemic of loneliness we create the possibility for offering empathy and community for those whose lives have been commodified by the neoliberal order. Empathy is not an invitation to passivity before strange worship; it is an invitation to resistance.

Empathy as Resistance?

Not all white Christian nationalists are victims in the neoliberal order. Many, in fact, benefit from the system and leverage its commodification of human souls toward their own interests. As Pamela Cooper-White argues, it is crucial to recognize that "empathy is not the same thing as sympathy."[34] In other words, offering empathy toward a white Christian nationalist does not mean we have to affirm their theology or worldview.

No one has explored this complex and challenging space more than author, podcaster, and stand-up actor Dylan Marron. Marron is a gay digital creator who made a video series called "Every Single Word," where he edited down popular films to only the words spoken by people of color.[35] For example, Marron's method

33. Arendt, *Origins of Totalitarianism,* 176.

34. Cooper-White, *Psychology of Christian Nationalism,* 107.

35. Marron details this experience in his TEDx talk "Empathy is Not Endorsement."

cut down the 558-minute *The Lord of the Rings* trilogy to forty-six seconds! As Marron posted this material to social media, he received vile, homophobic, and vicious comments from strangers that he filed away in what he calls a "HATE FOLDER."

After a profound interaction with an internet troll (I won't spoil the story for you), Marron began reaching out to people in his HATE FOLDER to see if they would be open to having a recorded conversation. In Marron's own words, "Sometimes the most subversive thing you could do was to speak with the people you disagreed with, and not simply at them."[36] Rather than engage in back and forth on social media (which rarely goes well!), Marron began messaging his internet haters and simply asking them: "Why did you write that?" The ensuing recorded conversations became a widely viewed podcast and now a book, titled, *Conversations with People Who Hate Me.*[37]

Marron's goal is to take "negative online comments and turn them into positive offline conversations that humanize the other."[38] The way Marron's empathy disorients enmity is breathtaking— some are even calling him the "Mr. Rogers of the internet." Underlying Marron's theory of change-making is his conviction that "Empathy is not endorsement" and that the internet "is not built to mitigate conflict; in fact, it seems like it's built to sustain it."[39] Marron is quick to acknowledge that empathy is "not a prescription for activism . . . some people don't feel safe talking to their detractors . . . and others feel so marginalized that they justifiably don't feel like they have any empathy to give."[40] This point is important: *not all of us are so privileged as to have conversations with people who hate us, and for some of us these conversations are not even safe.*

I recently had the opportunity to experiment with Marron's approach to vile social media comments. After I wrote a blog post on Christian nationalism and 9/11 for the Mennonite Church

36. Marron, "Empathy is Not Endorsement."

37. Marron, *Conversations with People Who Hate Me.*

38. Marron, "Empathy is Not Endorsement."

39. See Marron, *Conversations with People Who Hate Me,* 41 and 127–44.

40. Marron, "Empathy is Not Endorsement."

USA's "Cost of War" series, I received a vile comment by an internet stranger who questioned my faith and ended his rant by saying that "Menno Simons would be ashamed of you!" (Simons is a famous sixteenth-century Anabaptist and I teach at Anabaptist Mennonite Biblical Seminary). I chose not to respond publicly and immediately wrote him a private message on Facebook that said something like this:

> Dear so and so:
>
> I hope and pray that you're doing well. I don't believe we've met. I saw your comments on Facebook today about me. I'd be happy to have a conversation anytime about what it means to follow Jesus in this moment. Let me know if you're ever available. I'd be more than happy to talk on the phone or via Zoom.
>
> In Christ,
> Drew

When I woke up the next morning, the stranger had not responded to my message, but he did delete his comment. In some small way that private message was enough to humanize my dignity as a real, living person. Marron's work has taught me that empathy can be strategic and subversive. Empathy is a strategy of active resistance rather than passivity and deference. It can disorient enmity and polarization and create the conditions for peacebuilding. Most importantly, it is not an endorsement of our theological opponents' actions and beliefs, nor is it an invitation to hide our prophetic teeth. Rather, empathy is a way to create space for dialogue.

Dialogue Across Extreme Human Difference

Dialogue is a crucial tool for challenging Christian nationalism. The stakes are high. As Lisa Schirch and David Campt write, "In the next century, our very lives may depend on how well we as individuals, communities, and members of humanity can creatively address the challenges before us with tools of dialogue rather than with weaponry, coercion, or force."[41] The alternatives to dialogue are direct and cultural violence.

In the work and discipline of strategic peacebuilding, "dialogue" is a special term used to describe "a process for talking about tension-filled topics."[42] It is a "communication process that aims to build relationships between people as they share experiences, ideas, and information about common concerns."[43] In this sense, dialogue is different from "conversation, discussion, training or education and debate."[44] Rather than being merely a strategy of persuasion, dialogue focuses on building relationships with the presence of a trained facilitator. While "civility" and "impartiality" can be viable peacebuilding strategies, dialogue does not mean one has to soften their prophetic teeth or lean away from truth telling; rather, *shifting power* and *building relationship bridges* go together.[45] This point is especially important to remember for the church's role in challenging racial injustice and white supremacy.

A full-blown guide to facilitated dialogue is beyond the scope of this book. However, pastors and leaders are not without good and highly readable resources on this. I especially commend Lisa Schirch and David Campt's *The Little Book for Dialogue on Difficult Subjects* and, more recently, Pamela Cooper-White's *The Psychology of Christian Nationalism: Why People are Drawn In and How to Talk Across the Divide*.[46] Cooper-White's book, in particular, gives me hope as she pushes back on psychologists and journalists who have publicly argued that "you can't reason with a Trump supporter."

In contrast, Cooper-White interrogates the conscious and unconscious motivations that lead people to participate in cults

41. Schirch and Campt, *Dialogue for Difficult Subjects*, 78.

42. Schirch and Campt, *Dialogue for Difficult Subjects*, 5.

43. Schirch and Campt, *Dialogue for Difficult Subjects*, 6.

44. Schirch and Campt, *Dialogue for Difficult Subjects*, 6.

45. See especially Schirch, "Transforming the Colour of US Peacebuilding," 1–17.

46. See Schirch and Campt, *Dialogue for Difficult Subjects*; and Cooper-White, *The Psychology of Christian Nationalism*.

and the ways followers hand their conscience over to a strong man who promises to restore whatever is lacking in their lives. In this paradigm, the strong man is a father figure and narcissist who loves only himself, but his followers need the illusion of being loved by the strong man. Cooper-White argues that direct argument will almost never work with those hardened by "group think" since we are talking to an entire network (including Tucker Carlson, etc.) of right-wing propaganda, disinformation, and conspiracy theory that is hardened into the conscience through data saturation and confirmation bias.

To deprogram we must create pathways for recovery and sobriety, which includes reducing exposure to the strongman, his media empire, and, ultimately, changing the structural circumstances that led to radicalization (e.g., poverty, lack of community, third order suffering, etc.).

In contrast to direct argument, Cooper-White believes in "talk" or what she calls "triage" (which is just another word for dialogue). Cooper-White writes that "triage involves not only assessing how hardened the potential dialogue partner is in their beliefs, and who is the right messenger, but also assessing the context—is this the right time, the right place, the right social context in which to have such a discussion?"[47] Within this discernment she offers a helpful red, yellow and green light paradigm to minimize the potential for harm:

1. Red Light: STOP—talking will do no good—at least not here, not now, not by me.

2. Yellow light: Try but tread lightly.

3. Green light: Go deeper, gently and wisely.[48]

I found it freeing and encouraging that Cooper-White is also quick to acknowledge that not everyone is in a position to engage white Christian nationalists and that it's okay to say, "I disagree" and calmly walk away.

---

47. Cooper-White, *Psychology of Christian Nationalism*, 104.

48. Cooper-White, *Psychology of Christian Nationalism*, 105–24.

I think some congregations are strategically located to facilitate dialogue across human difference. Not every congregation will have the resources or bandwidth for this kind of work, but for those who do partnering with organizations like "The Colossian Forum" could offer hopeful pathways and trainings toward healing perception gaps between opposing groups.[49] One student in my resisting Christian nationalism class who lives in a rural corner of North Carolina is partnering with local churches to facilitate dinner groups of diverse people called "Common Ground." I like that. Having preemptive dialogue strategies in place, including safe and healthy exit plans, is crucial for Christians challenging Christian nationalism as we imagine how empathy and dialogue can be wielded to challenge white Christian nationalism.

The Spectrum of Allies

I will be the first to confess that I've had little luck challenging or evangelizing ambassadors of Christian nationalism in my social network through in-person dialogue or comment threads on social media. This might be one reason we should focus on dialogue with accommodators and discipling resisters and rejecters. In my moments of despair, I've also wondered if this type of toxic theology can only come out through prayer. I don't say this to sound hyperbolic or overly-religious—we need to pray!

I want to encourage us, however, to not think of full-scale conversion as the only option for bending the worldview of white Christian nationalists closer to Jesus and justice. Instead, I want to encourage us to think about shifting Christian nationalists' biblical convictions about key issues like immigration, gun violence, police brutality, structural racism, and so on so forth, one step toward resisters and rejecters of white Christian nationalism. No, this is not an invitation to become more liberal in the partisan political sense; rather, this is an invitation to become *more Christian*.

49. The Colossian Forum's mission is "to equip leaders to transform cultural conflicts into opportunities for spiritual growth and witness." See: https://colossianforum.org/.

54

One way to conceptualize these small shifts in loyalty comes from an organizing tool from George Lakey's concept of the "spectrum of allies."[50] Underlying this theory of change is the idea that "movements and campaigns are won not by overpowering one's active opposition, but by shifting each group one notch around the spectrum (passive allies into active allies, neutrals into passive allies, passive opponents into neutrals, and active opposition into passive opposition)."[51]

In the case of Christian nationalism, resisters into rejecters, accommodators into resisters, and ambassadors into accommodators. In the visual below, I've chosen to keep the spectrum of allies' neutrals category to signify what Anand Giridharadas calls "persuadables." Persuadables are American moderates who are "confused, torn, not sure which pole is their pole" and "do not hold fixed ideological positions on policy issues."[52] Too often we think of centrist Americans as holding a fixed ideological space when in fact they are malleable and persuadable. We can visualize these small shifts in loyalty as follows: [53]

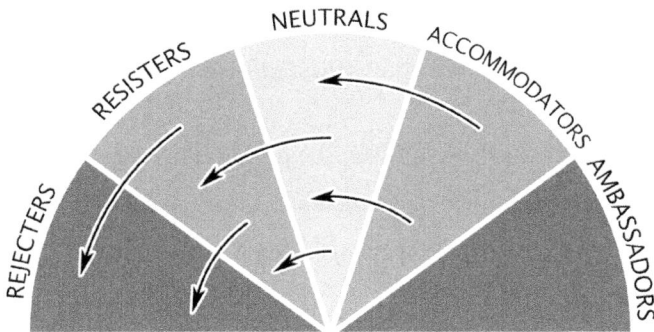

For me, the spectrum of allies is a helpful and more realistic way of framing conflict and social transformation. So often in Christian

50. See "Spectrum of Allies."
51. See "Spectrum of Allies."
52. Giridharadas, *Persuaders,* 220–21.
53. I'm grateful to Kajsa Herrstrom for creating this visual.

culture we think of full-scale conversion as the only way to transform our theological opponents and society at large. Yes, let's pray for and work toward conversion and repentance—but small shifts along the spectrum of allies around key issues through *empathy* and *dialogue* may prove to be a more effective way to change minds about God, power, race, and human difference.

So, how'd we get here? In short, we got here from evangelicals' quest for power and dominion over the US, neoliberalism's commodification of human souls, and social media's efficiency at spreading disinformation apart from reality and connectedness to traditional human collectives. As we live into this moment, empathy creates the potential for dialogue, and dialogue creates the possibility for theological transformation.

On this point we can formally end our "pause" and hit "play" for step four for challenging white Christian nationalism.

Questions for Reflection

1. How has social media impacted your relationships with family and friends?

2. In what ways have you witnessed disinformation spread on social media?

3. In what ways have you seen social media used for good?

4. How do you think social media has impacted congregations?

5. How has social media changed the ways people are theologically shaped and formed?

Chapter 4

What Is Political Idolatry and Why Is It Strange Worship?

There shall be no strange god among you; you shall not bow down
to a foreign god.

—PSALM 81:9

Idolatry at its roots is a misdirection of love and attention away
from God and toward something else that is not God.

—STEPHEN FOWL[1]

STEP FOUR IN CHALLENGING Christian nationalism is to name white Christian nationalism as a form of political idolatry. But what is an idol in the 2020s? This question is hard for us to answer today. We struggle to notice our idols today because most of the modern West doesn't openly worship at the feet of statues and offer sacrifice to deities in their temples. Perhaps the term *idol*, then, is dated, overly religious, and no longer useful for addressing the moment in which we are living? Or maybe it's not?

---

1. Fowl, *Idolatry*, 65.

The most important takeaway from recent scholarship on white Christian nationalism is that it has little to do with following the Jesus of the four Gospels and everything to do with preserving cultural privilege and political power, using Jesus and Christianity as mascots for coercing power over others. The primary object of white Christian Nationalists' worship is *power*—not the unarmed, self-emptying, boundary crossing, crucified Christ. In this sense, the word "idol" is an appropriate word for interrogating and understanding the spiritual and theological underpinnings of white Christian nationalism. That's because an idol is an object of power that distracts us from giving loyalty to God and God's ways in Jesus. An idol is an object of power that demands affection and loyalty. It is a competing allegiance to God.

In their classic book on idolatry in ancient Jewish thought, Moshe Halbertal and Avishai Margalit observe that the crux of idolatry is cognitive "error."[2] "Idolatry," they write, "is perceived first and foremost as an improper conception of God in the mind of the worshiper, thereby internalizing sin."[3] An idol, then, is an object of power that hijacks our theological imagination, distorts our knowledge of God and neighbor, and, ultimately, leads us into what the Jewish rabbis called "strange worship" (or, *avodah zarah*).

The emphasis on "knowledge" here is key: in ancient Jewish thought, idolatry was not something that merely occurred in your heart. Rather, idolatry was something that happened in your mind. *How we think about God matters. And how we think about our neighbors matters for how we think about God.*

This chapter offers an introduction to political idolatry in Jewish and early Christian thought. The goal is to offer biblical and theological resources for understanding strange worship today and to better recognize *when* and *how* political idolatry happens in the mind of the worshiper. Of equal concern is what communities can *do* to preemptively prevent strange worship before it happens.

A note to my readers: this chapter is an invitation to a biblical studies class in seminary. I invite you into a posture of curiosity

2. Halbertal and Margalit, *Idolatry*.
3. Halbertal and Margalit, *Idolatry*, 2.

about the ancient world. It might be helpful to grab a Bible and a cup of coffee or tea.

Strange Worship: A Short Introduction

It is important to recognize that Christians challenging Christian nationalism today are not the first generation of believers to negotiate political idolatry.[4] Israel, in fact, was birthed in the context of enslavement to Pharaoh in Egypt; the northern kingdom of Israel was exiled by Assyrian empire in 722 BCE, and the southern kingdom by Babylonian empire in 587 BCE. During the five-hundred-year period leading up to the birth of Jesus that we call Second Temple Judaism, the people of God lived under the rule of powerful warrior kings under the Greeks, Seleucids, Ptolemies and, finally, the Romans. Proclaiming loyalty to the one God was as much a political struggle as it was a theological one, as Jews lived out their loyalty to the Law of Moses *under* the yoke of foreign empires.

To this day, Yahweh's liberation of Israel out of Egypt in the Exodus narrative remains the most memorable moment of salvation in Jewish history. Jews celebrate this remarkable moment of rescue and deliverance during the Passover festival—a reminder that salvation is much more than personal salvation in Jewish thought. The books of Exodus and Deuteronomy narrate the miraculous Passover narrative, including images of Jews' oppression under empire (Exod 1:12–14), a deified king (Exod 7:9—11:10), and Yahweh's power to override empire's domination and injustice (Exod 12:1—18:27). Exodus and Deuteronomy also narrate how Israel became a people who worship one God without images. Indeed, Yahweh liberated Israel "out of Egypt from the house of slavery in order that Israel might worship no other gods but Yahweh alone" (Exod 20:2–3; Deut 5:6–7).

---

4. I am grateful to the *Mennonite Quarterly Review* for permission to republish part of Strait, "Political Idolatry and White Christian Nationalism" in this chapter.

Worshiping the one God was written into law when Moses received the Ten Commandments on Mt. Sinai. The first and second commandments infused Israel with a counter-cultural and, at times, anti-imperial vision of divinity and power. The first commandment (Exod 20:3; Deut 5:7) prohibited Israel from the worship of "other gods" (what scholars call monotheism). The second commandment (Exod 20:4–6; Deut 5:8–10) prohibited Israel from the artistic representation of the one God with precious materials like ivory, marble, stone, silver, and gold (what scholars call aniconicism). Monotheism is the worship of one God. Aniconicism is worship without images. Together, aniconic monotheism is the worship of one God without images of that God.

In ancient Judaism strange worship could happen in at least three ways: (1) the veneration of other gods or kings; (2) the veneration of gods' and kings' images with art; and (3) mistaken perceptions of power and divinity in the mind of the worshiper.[5] It is hard for us modern minds to understand this next point, but it is crucial to grasp: In the ancient world, there was not a distinction between politics and religion; the boundary between these spheres was porous. This is especially true in the ancient Near Eastern and Greco-Roman worlds, where all of life was structured around the worship of different gods and rulers that people venerated, sacrificed to, and prayed to in exchange for "benefits" like protection, peace, rain, happiness, healing, and so forth. These objects of power were thought of as "benefactors" and when honored, they could bestow "benefactions" or "benefits" on pious subordinates. In cities around the Mediterranean world that worshiped gods and kings, Israel's aniconic monotheism articulated a worldview that was . . . *strange* to its neighbors.

Jewish sensitivities to political idolatry can be felt from an early stage in its life together. As Carol A. Newsom observes, "Throughout the Hebrew Bible where the God of Israel is represented as having an opponent, this opponent is more often framed, not as another god, but as a human king."[6] To resist political

---

5. See Barclay, "Snarling Sweetly" 73–87.
6. Newsom, "God's Other," 31.

idolatry, eighth century BCE prophets such as Isaiah, followed by Nahum and Habakkuk, developed resistance literature to criticize the idols and cruel imperial policies of neighboring empires. Such criticism is felt in Isaiah, who was the first to attack foreign empire in the eighth century BCE: "[The Assyrian empire's] land is full of silver and gold, there is no limit to their treasures; their land is full of horses, there is no limit to their chariots. And their land is full of idols; they bow down to the work of their hand, to what their own fingers have wrought" (Isa 2:7–8). Moshe Weinfeld calls this literature "prophecies concerning empires," and Christopher B. Hays is certainly right in observing that when "one reads Isaiah, one is reading some of the world's oldest surviving resistance literature."[7] The struggle against idolatry, therefore, was intimately tied to Jews' negotiation of political authority.

In the Roman world, an ancient quotation from the Roman historian Tacitus (c. 56–120 CE) illustrates just how countercultural Jews' aniconic monotheism was for Roman onlookers. As I always tell my students, fifty words from an ancient source is better than two hundred from a modern source for understanding the biblical world. With some venom, Tacitus writes:

> The Egyptians worship many animals and monstrous images; the Jews conceive of one god only, and that with the mind alone: they regard as impious those who make from perishable materials representations of gods in man's image; that supreme and eternal being is to them incapable of representation and without end. Therefore they set up no statues in their cities, still less in their temples; this flattery is not paid their kings, nor this honour given to the Caesars. (*Hist.* 5.5.4, LCL)

Tacitus mocks Jews who do not erect statues to honor God, their own kings, and the Roman emperors. Under Roman power, Jews' cultural survival hinged on their ability to maintain their aniconic monotheism in a world full of emperor worship and political idolatry.

---

7. See Weinfeld, "Protest against Imperialism," 171; and Hays, "Isaiah as Colonized Poet," 51.

Jews' struggle for cultural survival can be felt even at the level of creative grammatical posturing. For example, to appease the worship of Roman emperors, Jews offered a sacrifice *to* Yahweh *on behalf* of Caesar (rather than *to* Caesar) twice a day in the Jerusalem temple.[8] When these sacrifices were suspended by Jewish revolutionaries in 66 CE, war broke out with Rome, resulting in the temple's destruction in 70 CE.

During this fraught period, there was a spectrum of Jewish sensitivities to and resistance strategies toward Roman power that included assimilation, accommodation, violent resistance, rationalizing imperial domination, resistance literature, apocalyptic theologies of resistance, banditry, terrorism, public wailing, prayer and penitence, pacifist foot dragging, strategic nonviolence, and the articulation of alternative cosmic hierarchies that subordinate the gentile angry tyrant to Israel's God.[9] While not all Jews agreed on *when* political idolatry happens, the creative capacity to negotiate and, at times, resist political idolatry was a regular feature of Jews' life together under Roman power during the decades leading up to and after the life of Jesus.

I think Jewish and early Christian negotiation of political idolatry offers us wisdom today for challenging power worship. The political metaphor of idolatry provides an especially neglected tool for interrogating the power dynamics of white Christian nationalism and its misdirected loyalties. Its neglect is felt in that political idolatry is not discussed in any significant way in a single major Bible dictionary entry on "idolatry" that seminary students, pastors, and Bible professors use in libraries around the world.[10]

If one thinks that idolatry only happens in the sphere of religion, then the veneration of a political system or a partisan

---

8. See Josephus, *J.W.* 2.197; *Ag. Ap.* 2.76–77, 409–10, 412–17; Philo, *Legat.* 317; see also *Legat.* 157, 291; *Flacc.* 48–49.

9. See Strait, *Hidden Criticism of the Angry Tyrant,* 125–33.

10. But see now Strait, "Idols, Idolatry," 467–469. I'm grateful to my Bible department assistant, Anna Ressler, for helping me investigate essays on idolatry in Bible dictionaries.

allegiance is of no concern. The people of God must rethink the boundaries of the political metaphor for this moment.

The Political Metaphor of Idolatry

Ancient Jews had two metaphors for understanding idolatry. The first metaphor is called the marital metaphor of idolatry. The marital metaphor is binary, or black and white, and it tends to dominate our modern understandings of idolatry. In this metaphor, God is perceived as a husband who is in an exclusive covenant relationship with Israel, the wife. The marital metaphor is patriarchal and in some Old Testament texts misogynistic. When Israel worships another god, she fornicates with a third partner and thereby commits adultery/idolatry against God. It can be visualized like this:

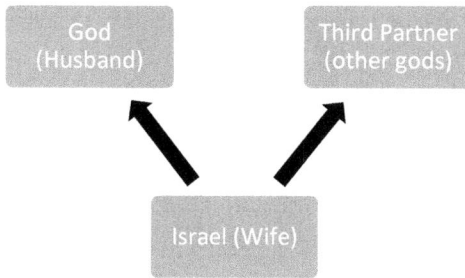

God
(Husband)

Third Partner
(other gods)

Israel (Wife)

The black and white nature of the marital metaphor cannot account for the complexity of gestures toward political authority that can lead to idolatry. To interrogate the gestures that lead to political idolatry, ancient Jews drew on a different metaphor that we call the political metaphor of idolatry.

The political metaphor is more complex than the marital metaphor. Instead of a black and white model of discernment, it adopts a triangular model to interrogate the boundaries of political power. In the political metaphor, the threatening third party is the veneration of political authorities (including kings, queens, or presidents) and the veneration of political institutions (including the military, economy, or even taxation). One sectarian Jewish movement called the Fourth Philosophy during the time of Jesus even believed that paying taxes to Caesar was an act of betrayal and political idolatry.[11] In the political metaphor, the threatening third party could also be royal ideologies—or discourses of power that distract us from giving loyalty to God alone.

In contrast to the binary nature of the marital metaphor, the political metaphor is "divisible" in the sense that God can share power with a subordinate human ruler (Jer 27:12–13; Isa 44:24–28; 45:1, 14; 1 Esd 2:3). In this model, a human doesn't have to fornicate with a third partner to commit idolatry. Instead, the human can simply "take" or even "transfer" the sovereignty of God to oneself, hence the problem of deification.[12] Deification is when humans glorify and worship a human as a god.

Jewish sensitivities to the problem of deification are felt especially when Israel transitioned from a theocracy to a monarchy. Such sensitivities are felt in the book of Judges when Israel was ruled by tribal chieftains and the people of God started grumbling for a human king "to be like the other nations" (1 Sam 8:5; 10:17–19; 12:12). Notwithstanding Samuel's warnings against life under a human king (1 Sam 8:11–17), the Israelites were "determined to have a king" so that "they may be like the other nations" (1 Sam 8:19–20). Israel's ensuing transition to a monarchy from 1000–586 BCE raised difficult questions about how to place limitations on the Israelite king's power so that he does not become glorified and venerated as a god.

To put limitations on the Israelite king's power, the author(s) of Deuteronomy composed the "Law of the King" to prohibit the Israelite king from a path toward deification. Specifically, the Law of the King portrays the ideal Israelite king as one who does not accumulate weapons, women, and wealth (Deut 17:14–19). The king was also required to read the "Law of the King" daily to "not exalt himself above other members of the community" (Deut 17:20). The "Law of the King" democratized Israel's monarchy and may reflect the only attempt to place limitations on a king's power in the ancient Near East.

11. See Josephus, *Ant.* 18.23–24; *J.W.* 2.118, 425; Acts 5:36–37.

12. Halbertal and Margalit, *Idolatry*, 220, 228.

At the core of the political metaphor is God's political sovereignty and exclusivity as Creator, Lord, King, Mother, Savior, and so on. We can visualize the political metaphor of idolatry in the following way:

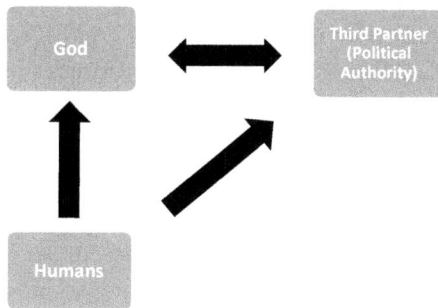

The primary question that the political metaphor addresses is: How exclusive is God's political sovereignty? Is loyalty to one's country an act of betrayal? What gestures toward political authority lead to betrayal? And at what point does loyalty to political authority become a distraction from our loyalty to God? I will return to these difficult questions at the end of this chapter.

To summarize, idolatry is a mistaken perception and understanding of God in our minds. An idol is a distraction; it is an object of power that distorts our knowledge of God and neighbor. Idols, including political power, are a competing loyalty that can make certain demands of affection and loyalty on human subjects. Learning how to negotiate these demands in responsible ways is the task of every Christian generation as we publicly express our loyalty to God in ever-changing political contexts. Jesus also experienced these competing loyalties, and we can learn from his example.

Jesus and Political Idolatry

The "render to Caesar" passage in Matthew (22:21) offers us a glimpse into Jesus' attitude toward state power. The influence of the saying in early Christianity is evident by its popularity (see

Mark 12:17; Matt 22:21; Luke 20:25; Gos. Thom. 100:2–4; and possibly Rom 13:7). But if the history of interpretation is any indication, interpreters cannot agree on what the saying means. The saying is admittedly ambiguous; the danger for all interpreters is manipulating the saying to align with our personal politics.

To interpret the "render to Caesar" riddle responsibly, we need to know a thing or two about Jews' attitudes toward Roman taxation. Since the time when Rome pacified Israel in 63 BCE, Israel paid tribute to Rome, a symbolic gesture of its subordinate status. Naturally, the payment was offensive and burdensome to many, and so created a conundrum for Jews: one could pay the tribute while internally dragging their feet, or one could openly resist payment through violent revolution. We have examples of both strategies of imperial negotiation. The perennial danger for the dissident voice was to not irk Rome's military into violent repression. In 6–9 CE, for example, a dissident named Judas the Galilean led a movement to resist Roman tribute because only "God was their Lord" (Josephus, *War* 2.117–118; Acts 5:37). For Judas and his followers, paying the tribute was a competing allegiance to God—an act of political idolatry.

It is between these Jewish dispositions of loyalty, accommodation, or violent retaliation against Rome, that the Pharisees and accommodationist Herodians wish to entrap Jesus. Recognizing their intent, Jesus asks to see the coin used for the tax. The fact that Jesus wasn't carrying one may reflect his own sensitivities to the first and second commandments (Exod 20:4–5). One ancient author even reports that the sectarian Jewish group called the Essenes refused to carry, behold, or fashion an image (Hipp. *Haer.* 9.21). The Roman denarius shown to Jesus, after all, had an image of the emperor with divine features—hence, Jesus' question: "Whose head is this and whose title?" (Matt 22:20).

Hundreds of these denarii have survived from the ancient world. If the denarius is from the reign of the emperor Tiberius (14–37 CE), it was stamped with the inscription: "Tiberius Caesar, son of the deified Augustus, [himself] Augustus." On the reverse side of the coin was a seated woman who represented the goddess

Pax (or Rome's "peace"). Surrounding the woman is the inscription, *PONTIFEX MAXIMUS*, or "High Priest." Taken together, these images and inscriptions evoke an idolatrous image of the emperor's superhuman status and peace through strength.

So far so good. It isn't until Jesus responds to the image of Caesar that we run into interpretive problems. The trap is set—if Jesus says don't pay the tax, he will be painted into a corner as an insurrectionist. If he says do pay the tax, he will be painted into a corner as an accommodationist or, worse yet, an idolater. In a world where criticism of Rome could evoke retaliation, Jesus responds with intentional ambiguity of expression: "Give therefore to Caesar the things that are Caesar's and to God the things that are God's" (Matt 22:21).

Already in the exchange, Jesus minimizes Caesar's image and power after they hand him the denarius by asking, "Whose head is this, and whose title?" (Matt 22:20). Ha! Everyone and their dog already know who is on the coin. Jesus' question diminishes Caesar's power, a point animated by the tension between "the things of Caesar" and "the things of God." Any serious Jew in the first century knew where their loyalties resided since they would have believed that everything belonged to God, including earthly rulers. Jesus' answer, then, offered them a handrail for living faithfully with one foot in the kingdom of God and one foot in the kingdoms of this world. Jesus was saying, sure, pay back the denarius to the mortal Caesar, but ultimately your whole life belongs to God (and so does Caesar's).

For Christians today, the riddle invites a posture of suspicion toward ruling powers rather than passive trust. For Matthew's Jesus, "You can't serve both God and money" (Matt 6:24). Herein lies the problem with Christian nationalism in the United States: its loyalty to the things of Caesar too often supersedes the things of God. Christian devotion to the things of Caesar remains an ongoing threat to democracy and the church's public witness in the US.

A contemporary example for how Christian nationalism lords the things of Caesar over the US can be found in recent "In God We Trust" bills. In 1956 the US national motto was changed from

E. Pluribus Unum (out of many, one) to "In God We Trust." The new law, signed by President Dwight D. Eisenhower, mandated that all US currency bear the new religious motto. At the time, the mandate was intended to differentiate Americans' purported religious piety from Russia's communist atheism, despite the motto's ambiguous object—indeed, trust in whose God? Litigation against the motto's potential infringement on the first amendment ultimately failed, opening the door for Christian nationalists to claim the ambiguous motto as their own in a bid to make America a Christian nation.

More recently, the right-wing coalition "Project Blitz" has sought to "blitz" the country with "In God We Trust" bills to placard the motto on license plates, state capitols, and public school classrooms.[13] Recently, Texas joined a dozen other states that now require the national motto to be displayed in public schools.[14] In July of 2021, city council members in Chesapeake, Virginia passed a proposal to emblazon every city-owned car and truck with the motto at a cost of $87,000 to taxpayers.[15] These seemingly pious moves are seen by political operatives on the religious right as an incremental strategy to pass bigger legislation on issues that privilege conservative white Christian values.

The perennial danger of the things of Caesar in a modern democracy is this: it can be leveraged for the common good, or it can be leveraged to pacify difference and lord power over others.

MAGA Superstition

Political idolatry may be sneaky and seemingly innocuous, but its effects on human collectives are no less devastating. Once you see political idolatry, you can't unsee it. Like Paul's distress over Athens' city of idols in Acts 17, we can responsibly paraphrase his

13. See Taylor, "In God We Trust."
14. See Lopez, "Texas Public School."
15. See Rago, "In God We Trust Decals."

dismay: "Americans, I see how extremely superstitious (*deisidaimonia*) you are in every way!" (Acts 17:22).

Political superstition, or *deisidaimonia* in Greek, runs deep in the veins of Christian nationalism. For Luke and Greco-Roman philosophers, *deisidaimonia* evoked faith by fear, a neurotic obsession with the divine, public stunts of pious ostentation, and defective knowledge of the divine. It's tempting to think that modern societies have special immunity from superstition, but we don't. If you don't believe me, take a few minutes to watch images and videos of the January 6 Capitol insurrection. The Capitol insurrection is one of the greatest public stunts of religious ostentation in American history as self-proclaimed Christians prayed and sang to Jesus, bore life-size crosses, prophesied, and performed exorcisms—all while violently laying siege to the center of American democracy.

Many of these images and videos have been archived through a partnership between the University of Alabama's Department of Religious Studies and the Smithsonian National Museum of American History.[16] Two specific images from the insurrection still distress me. The first is of an insurrectionist holding a large poster of white Jesus with a "Make America Great Again" (MAGA) hat on.[17] The other is of multiple videos of insurrectionists singing praise songs and praying their way into the capitol adorned with MAGA gear and American flags.[18] Christian nationalism is a form of superstition. It is superstitious because, instead of appealing to the God of all nations, it appeals to a culturally fabricated God for cultural privilege, power, and benefits, while denying these same benefits to others (e.g., persons of color, immigrants, and LGBTQ+ persons, among others).

16. Images and videos from the January 6 insurrection have been archived by the University of Alabama's Department of Religious Studies and the Smithsonian's National Museum of American History on a website titled, "Uncivil Religion."

17. See https://uncivilreligion.org/home/media/maga-jesus.

18. For multiple examples caught on video, see https://uncivilreligion.org/home/rituals.

When one studies images and videos from the January 6 insurrection, it becomes clear that many of these insurrectionists were having a religious and spiritual experience—perhaps even a "mountain top experience." A good example of this is the right-wing Texas "Three Percenters" recruiter Guy Reffit. Reffit is charged with leading the pro-Trump mob into Congress. After the insurrection, Reffit texted a friend: "I got hit with rubber bullets and pepper sprayed. I was the first person to light the fire on the Capitol steps . . . WE TOOK THE CAPITAL . . . I was willing to die. I had a very epic point in my life, actually."[19]

When Reffit returned to Texas he bragged to his three children and showed them videos of his role in the insurrection. Reffit's only son, a nineteen-year-old, was not amused, so a few days later Reffit warned his children that "traitors get shot." Despite the violent warning, Reffit's son met with the FBI to turn his father in. While taking the stand, Reffit's son brought his father to tears as he testified against him in support of the prosecutors' charge of five felony counts. Strikingly, Reffit's son acknowledged that he felt "gross" and "very uncomfortable" but that his relationship with his father became polarized after 2016 and that "it would be a good thing to talk about for a lot of families that are going through this . . . There were hundreds of people on January 6, they all had families. Everyone is attached to them."[20]

This story is gut-wrenching. Misinformation and conspiracy theories, in this case the idea of a stolen election, have torn apart and traumatized whole families. The radicalization of Reffit reflects the ways that idols can become "creatures of the human imagination that take control of people and their lives, and the breaking of idols means the uncovering of the fictional and illusive character of these creatures of the imagination."[21] Anyone who has had serious conversations with Christian nationalists knows the depths of control these fictional and allusive creatures hold

19. See Cabral and McKelvey, "Guy Reffit."
20. Hsu, "Rage Met by Revulsion."
21. See Halbertal and Margalit, *Idolatry*, 6.

over communities and family members. One of these creatures is what I am calling MAGA Jesus.

MAGA Jesus is perhaps best exemplified in the prayer prayed on the Senate floor by the horn studded Capitol insurrectionist Jacob Chansley, otherwise known as "QAnon Shaman." The prayer is worth quoting in full. As you read it, I want you to seriously ask: If idolatry is something that happens in the mind of the worshiper, then who is Mr. Chansley praying to in Christ's holy name?

> Jesus Christ, we invoke your name! Thank you, heavenly Father, for gracing us with this opportunity. For this opportunity to stand up for our unalienable rights. Thank you, Heavenly Father, for being the inspiration needed to these police officers to allow us into this building . . . to allow us to send a message to all the tyrants, the communists, and the globalists that this is our nation and not theirs. That we will not allow the American way of the USA to go down. Thank you, divine, omniscient, and omnipresent creator God, for filling this chamber with your white light and love, with your white light of harmony. Thank you for filling this chamber with patriots who love you and that love Christ. Thank you for blessing every one of us who is here now. Thank you, divine creator God, for surrounding us with divine, omnipresent, white light of love, protection, peace, and harmony. Thank you for allowing the USA to be reborn . . . We love you, and we thank you. In Christ's holy name we pray. Amen [to loud cheers].[22]

For anyone conversant with the aims and teachings of Jesus, the prayer's divine object reflects an unrecognizable deity who divinely inspired a violent siege by white supremacists to save America from imagined decline. The prayer communicates several things that I find striking. First, it implies that God inspired the police officers to "allow" the insurrectionists into the Capitol building. Second, it implies that America is on the brink of collapse. Third, it suggests that the chamber is filled with "patriots"—not

22. I transcribed the prayer from Mogelson, "Reporter's Video from Inside the Capitol Siege."

disciples, missionaries, or evangelists. Fourth, it suggests that America is being "born again."

When I evaluate this prayer with congregations, someone in the audience always points out the three occurrences of "white light." What's up with that? The collective wisdom of audiences I've spoken with tend to associate it with racialized overtones. The prayer reflects how idols can distort our knowledge of God *and* neighbor—indeed, "this is our nation and not theirs." One can pray in the name of Jesus Christ, but that doesn't always mean that one is praying to Jesus Christ.

I don't say this to sound provocative, but I think that MAGA Jesus can be found in the Bible. MAGA Jesus is what ancient Jews called in Greek an *eidōlon* —or an "idol." In the ancient world, an *eidōlon* meant a "shadow," a "phantom," or something that "appears" or merely "seems to be." The first century Jewish philosopher Philo from Alexandria, Egypt, writes this of *eidōlon*: "These are the things which Moses calls idols (*eidōla*), resembling shadows and phantoms" (*Leg.* 1.25). In carefully choosing this Greek word, the people of God resisted superstition and objects of power, both real and imagined, that could distort one's knowledge of God.

The problem, then, is not whether Christian nationalists are having a genuine religious experience when they pray in the name of Jesus Christ—they are! The problem is that the object of their worship is a shadow cast by white grievance toward a perceived loss of cultural power and privilege. This is why MAGA Jesus is a form of *avodah zarah*, or "strange worship." As Willie Jennings argues, "This is why nationalism for us moderns is the first idolatry because it places another god before God. It places a god-bound-to-our-nation over the God of all nations . . . The horror of the god-bound-to-us nationalism is not that it wants our respect; it wants our desire."[23] Desire for power. Desire for order. Desire for boundaries and walls. Desire for whiteness. Desire for wealth. Desire for "law and order." The object of these desires is *not* God; rather, it is power and privilege.

23. Jennings, *Acts,* 22–23.

The Idol of Whiteness

Desire for idols, according to theologian Stephen Fowl, "does not need to be extinguished, but rightly directed."[24] To rightly direct our desire toward love of God and neighbor in this political moment we need to talk more about whiteness, a concept I defined in chapter 2. I invite you to sit with this section in a posture of curiosity and openness.

Recently, PRRI released new data about "Anti-Black Racism" in the US. Among adherents of Christian nationalism, 57 percent disagree that white supremacy remains a problem in the US (compared to 65 percent of Americans who agree). They found that 70 percent of adherents of Christian nationalism disagree that "generations of slavery and discrimination have created conditions that make it difficult for many Black Americans to work their way out of the lower class." Disagreement with this statement rises to 83 percent among white adherents of Christian nationalism.[25] This survey data paints a stark portrait of the ways white Christian nationalism whitewashes structural inequalities and historical inequities in favor of a "color blind" worldview where all Americans purportedly operate on an equal playing field.

The racial progress narrative that has led to the idea that "all lives matter" is a powerful myth among white Christian nationalists, including among those who reside within its softer versions. Scholars like Michelle Alexander, Anthea Butler, W. E. B. Dubois, Jemar Tisby, among others, have dissected this myth for us. Suffice it to say that *we do not live on an equal playing field.* The United States is founded on the free labor of enslaved Africans and a genocide against Native Americans; this is our original sin, and its effects are ongoing by intelligent design.[26]

24. Fowl, *Idolatry*, 66.

25. See "Christian Nation?"

26. Take income inequality as one example. In 2018, the average chief executive of an S&P 500 company made 287 times more than their median employee. Some 85.7 percent of these wealthy executives are white and only 5.9 percent of them are Black. On the ground, white women make 79 cents for every dollar a man makes. Black women, 64 cents. Multiracial women, 63

The intelligent design that codes inequality into our social fabric is programmed by whiteness. In chapter 2 I adopted Willie James Jennings' definition of whiteness as "a way of imagining oneself as the central facilitating reality of the world . . . and Whiteness is having the power to realize and sustain that imagination."[27] When whiteness is threatened, its worshipers fight back through a politics of contempt, coercion, and even direct violence. Whiteness, in this sense, demands loyalty to maintain or even improve one's social status in society at the expense of one's neighbor. Whiteness distracts us from loving God and neighbor.

The Rev. Dr. Andrew T. Draper asks, "How does one worship Whiteness?" Draper suggests, "By seeking to become like it, by assimilating to its form, by being enamored with its power, and by internalizing its standards of beauty and rationality."[28] Draper's point reminds us that whiteness isn't merely about skin pigment. Even persons of color can assimilate to its form and be enamored with its power. Just think of Supreme Court justice Clarence Thomas who frequently rules against the interests of African Americans. White Christian nationalism is a movement that is not just enamored with white power, but invites all of society to assimilate to and internalize its values of "MAGA Jesus and country," even if that means by way of coercion.

The idol of whiteness is about control and mastery, not freedom and personal rights. Whiteness is rooted in the US's original sin, and it continues to pacify anyone who doesn't get in line by coercion, law, or the disciplinary power of incarceration. Because Christians have become a vector for whiteness in the United States, Draper suggests that white Christians need to undergo an intentional "de-conversion" process from our baptism into the habits of whiteness that lead to racism and power worship. Draper offers five steps for this work of de-conversion:

---

cents. And Native American women, 60 cents. It takes women an extra forty-two days of work to make what a man did in 2020. See Bleiweis et al., "Women of Color and the Wage Gap."

27. Jennings, "To be a Christian Intellectual."

28. See Draper, "End of 'Mission,'" 178.

1. Repentance for complicity in systemic sin.

2. Learning from theological and cultural resources not our own.

3. Choosing to locate our lives in places and structures in which we are necessarily guests.

4. Tangible submission to non-White ecclesial leadership.

5. Hearing and speaking the glory of God in unfamiliar cadences.[29]

Draper's suggestions offer us a kind of modern-day nonviolent iconoclasm (iconoclasm is the rejection or destruction of religious images or idols). What I mean is a nonviolent strategy to decenter and, ultimately, dismantle the idol of whiteness in our congregations. I won't pretend that we can invite ambassadors and accommodators of white Christian nationalism into that work now. But with resisters and rejecters? That work can begin now.

To challenge the idols of neighboring empires, ancient Jews developed a literary device that was re-purposed from one generation to the next. That device is the portrayal of the idol artisan who creates a lifeless image of the divine out of gold, silver and stone, but in reality is only projecting him/herself onto the lifeless image (Isa 44:9–20; Wis 15:16–17; Acts 17:25). So the Psalmist: "Those who make them [idols] and all who trust them shall become like them" (Ps 135:18). While we no longer worship and sacrifice at the altar of many gods, we are no less superstitious than ancient persons. Whiteness is a form of superstition—an idol we fabricate out of fear and desire to control, dominate, and accumulate wealth over others. That's what is so dangerous about the religion of whiteness: when it is worshiped, its values of control and mastery become our own.

---

29. Draper, "End of 'Mission,'" 181.

A Process, Not a Moment

"I got caught up in the moment." These are the words of Capitol insurrectionist Josiah Colt from Idaho who was memorably photographed swinging from the Senate balcony onto the floor. According to reports, Colt and his two companions showed up to the insurrection with multiple weapons, including a pistol, ammunition magazines, body armor, bear mace, knives, and a taser gun ready for a "boogaloo" (a right-wing code word for civil war).[30]

When idolaters of power are "caught up in the moment," there's no turning back. This is a reminder that the events leading up to getting "caught up in the moment" are what matter the most, pastorally speaking. According to the PIRUS database (Profiles of Individual Radicalization in the United States), radicalization is a slow process that, on average, takes five or more years.[31] Disturbingly, among QAnon conspiracy theorists who've committed violent crimes, the process of radicalization is accelerated to a matter of weeks or months (64 percent of QAnon offenders radicalized in less than one year).[32] I did some internet sleuthing and can't find much on Mr. Colt's life, but I suspect that there are a number of small, seemingly harmless events in his life that led to the moment of hanging from the Senate balcony with tactical gear on. The theologian Stephen Fowl best captures this dynamic and is worth quoting in full:

> idolatry is the result of a number of small incremental moves: a set of seemingly benign or even prudent decisions; a set of habits and dispositions—often acquired through subtle participation in a wider culture; a set of influential friendships. All of these work in complex combinations gradually to direct our attention slowly and almost imperceptibly away from the one true God towards that which is not God.[33]

30. See McDonald, "Man Who Swung."

31. Schirch, "Mapping the Ecology of Violent Extremism," 23.

32. See "START, National Consortium for the Study of Terrorism and Responses to Terrorism."

33. Fowl, *Idolatry*, 4.

Idolatry, in this sense, is not always the result of a singular moment or decision. It is, rather, a slow process and set of decisions and dispositions that build on one another until we get "caught up in the moment."

Fowl warns that the Old Testament prophets were not very successful at changing the minds of idolaters who got caught up in the moment. While we probably can't expect to be more successful today than the biblical prophets were, we live out our faithfulness by practicing preventative medicine by focusing on the habits and dispositions that resist idolatry in the first place.

At least six postures and dispositions toward political authority lead to strange worship; together, they provide a starting point for thinking critically about how we negotiate and engage our current political climate. Loyalty to political power becomes strange worship and an idolatrous third partner when:

1. Loyalty to political authority undermines our exclusive loyalty to the life and teachings of Jesus.

2. Loyalty to political authority inspires and/or celebrates harm toward our neighbors.

3. Loyalty to political authority sees our country—rather than the unarmed, multicultural church—as the primary context for Christian action, mission, and witness.

4. Pledging loyalty to one's country supersedes the value we place on our baptismal identity.

5. Loyalty to political authority stimulates a hierarchical ethno-racial caste system—an "us" vs. "them" worldview and purity culture.

6. Christians approach partisan political loyalties with a posture of absolute or deferent trust rather than ambivalence and suspicion.

In naming some of the dispositions and gestures that lead to political idolatry—or getting "caught up in the moment"—I hope to offer Christians challenging Christian nationalism a more descriptive framework for naming the boundaries of the political metaphor of idolatry today. In so doing, I hope to do two things. First, to offer a modest handrail for naming *when* and *how* political power can coopt and hijack our theological imagination. Second, to redirect our "gaze" away from the allure of the idols of whiteness, fear, and violence and toward the God who made a public spectacle of politics through coercion by rising from the dead on a Roman cross, an instrument of Roman political pacification.[34]

In chapter 7 I will return to follow Fowl's lead in naming specific habits and dispositions Christians can adopt to resist political idolatry in community.

A Note about Loving Idolaters

Are all ambassadors and accommodators of white Christian nationalism idolaters of power? I don't know—I'm not God. One thing I do know is that the God we serve, who was incarnated in Jesus of Nazareth, is a God who "desires those who desire idols."[35] As pastors and leaders challenging white Christian nationalism, we must never forget that the objects of our resistance are also an object of God's love and desire.

Step four for challenging Christian nationalism is to name Christian nationalism as political idolatry.

Questions for Reflection

1. Is political idolatry a new concept to you? How so? How not?

2. What stands out to you in the QAnon Shaman's prayer on the Senate floor?

3. Where do you see political idolatry at work in your community?

---

34. On American Christian nationalism's idols of power, fear, and violence, see Whitehead, *American Idolatry*.

35. Jennings, *Acts*, 176.

4. Of the six postures that lead to political idolatry, which one stands out to you the most?

5. How can congregations and Christians find spaces to talk more about political idolatry?

Chapter 5

Why the Way of Jesus?

You pore over the scriptures for you imagine that you will find
eternal life in them. And all the time they give their testimony
to me!

—JESUS (JOHN 5:39)

We live in a Bible-haunted nation.

—KAITLYN SCHIESS[1]

IF THE JANUARY 6 Capitol insurrection is any indication, the Bible
was a source of inspiration for political violence and strange worship as insurrectionists sang worship songs to Jesus, read Scripture
publicly, blew shofars, waved Bibles over their heads, performed
exorcisms, and carried placards of "white Jesus with a MAGA hat
on" as they sought to violently overturn a democratic election.
Even President Trump once boasted that, "No one reads the Bible
more than me."[2]

The Bible matters among white Christian nationalists—even
while the movement politicizes key teachings in the Bible on

1. Schiess, *Bible and the Ballot*, 1.
2. For the quote's context, see Zaimov, "Donald Trump."

justice and loving one's neighbor as leftist "woke" propaganda. Recent data by PRRI legitimates this impulse. When Americans were asked whether biblical injunctions about taking care of the poor were primarily about charitable acts by individuals or our obligation to create a just society, about two-thirds of adherents and sympathizers of white Christian nationalism chose the former.[3]

I believe that the way of Jesus is our best antidote to strange worship. I don't make this statement to sound overly pious or to virtue signal my spiritual credentials. Jesus is a jarring figure whose life and teachings challenge the worst impulses of Christians across the political and theological spectrum. Step five for challenging white Christian nationalism is to preach the whole life of Jesus. By "whole life" I mean the "whole gospel" of Jesus' birth, life and teachings, death, resurrection, ascension, and return.

One would think that step five is self-evident for all Christians. It's not. Christian nationalists tend to emphasize the salvation and eternal life (or judgment!) that Jesus brings, but his teachings and *way of life* are peripheral, misunderstood, explained away, or, ironically, deemed offensive. The task ahead for Christians challenging Christian nationalism is to figure out how to shift idolatrous loyalties toward power worship and to reorient those loyalties around the life and teachings of Jesus.

In this way, effective resistance against white Christian nationalism is a contestation over the Bible's meaning and the kind of world it invites its hearers to nurture. Biblical interpretation matters for this moment. In fact, the Bible might be one of the biggest stumbling blocks for human progress around questions of climate change, cultural violence, immigration, incarceration, racial justice, militarism, LGBTQ+ rights, and so on so forth. How do we leverage biblical interpretation responsibly, effectively, and *publicly* to challenge white Christian nationalism?

This chapter unpacks this question and offers pastors and leaders tools for challenging white Christian nationalism with the way of Jesus.

---

3. See "Christian Nation?"

Christian Nationalism and the Bible

On June 1, 2020, US Park Police and Bureau of Prisons officers used pepper spray and tear gas to clear protesters from Lafayette Square near the White House. After much confusion, government watch dogs reported that the Trump administration did not order the confrontation, but Trump expressed interest in visiting the site within hours of the operation. The ensuing photo-op of President Trump holding a Bible in front of a church remains one of the most memorable images from the Trump presidency. For some Christians, including me, the spectacle captured a chilling juxtaposition of Christianity's sacred text alongside an aspiring authoritarian. In contrast, for Christian nationalists, the image captured the purported piety and power of a president who wished to impose so-called "biblical values" on Americans' life together.

The political spectacle in Lafayette Square illustrates just how deep the Bible runs in our national consciousness and body politic. A key predictor of ambassadors of white Christian nationalism is belief in the Bible, including belief in the Bible as the literal word of God and as perfectly true (59 percent of ambassadors of Christian nationalism claim to read Scripture weekly or more and 50 percent say they read the Bible literally).[4] Sociologists have found that there is a strong correlation between biblical literalism (otherwise known as *biblicism*) and Christian nationalism, and biblical literalists are more likely to embrace conspiracy theories and to hold negative views of science.[5]

White Christian nationalism's biblical literalism creates an uncomfortable reality for Christians challenging Christian nationalism. One of the few shared values between Christian nationalists and Christians challenging Christian nationalism is a shared value of the Bible's authority for making sense of salvation and Christian discipleship. Both sides appeal to the same Bible for moral

---

4. See Whitehead and Perry, *Taking America Back for God,* 12; and Table 1.2 on p. 30.

5. See Baker et al., "Crusading for Moral Authority," 587–607; and Walker and Vegter, "Christ, Country, and Conspiracies?" 1–15.

guidance, yet both sides interpret the Bible with vastly different outcomes and visions of belonging and human flourishing. Biblicism remains a major stumbling block for challenging Christian nationalism.

Before I talk more about resisting Christian nationalism with the way of Jesus, we need to stop and clear some brush off the path of biblical interpretation that leads to the way of Jesus. This brush is thick and thorny and is entangled in how we use and read the Bible. We are living in a moment of cultural foment where the Bible is not only a contested document but is regularly used to legitimate harm toward our neighbors. I offer three cautions for reflection.

Caution #1: The Bible is not an object of Christian worship. The Bible is not a fourth member of the Trinity. As Christians, the object of our worship is the God of Israel incarnated in Jesus Christ. Another way of thinking about this is to say that the Bible is the words of God about the Word of God—being Jesus of Nazareth. You see what I did there? In the Christian tradition we worship Jesus Christ as mediated through Scripture and not the Bible itself. The Bible points us toward God. As Christian Smith argues, "It is Jesus Christ—and not the Bible—who is 'the image of the invisible God' (Col 1:19)."[6]

Caution #2: Anytime the Bible is used to lord power over others it is being used not as an authoritative text but as an authoritarian text. Biblical authoritarianism—especially white male biblical authoritarianism—presents an immediate threat to our climate, persons of color and Jewish communities, and the full inclusion of women and our queer neighbors in church and society. Put more bluntly, if you love your doctrine of Scripture more than your neighbor you might be a bibliolater (which is a person who worships the Bible rather than the God the Bible points toward). As Angela Parker has recently shown, biblical authority for white Christian nationalists is often code for white supremacist biblical authoritarianism, where the Bible serves "not as a conversation

---

6. Smith, *Bible Made Impossible,* 117.

starter but as a conversation ender" and the "biblical text becomes a bludgeoning tool used to exert supremacist authoritarianism."[7]

Caution #3: When the Bible is not interpreted in community, or with accountability to a community, bad things happen. We are living in a moment of polarization and misinformation peddled by charlatans and celebrity pastors and politicians who publicly interpret the Bible for the masses. Meanwhile, consumers peddle biblical memes and pedantic interpretations of the Bible inside of information silos on a mass scale through social media. This is dangerous and leads to biblical interpretation that lacks accountability. Reading the Bible in community disorients biblical authoritarianism and holds our readings of Scripture accountable—it also leaves room for the Holy Spirit to speak!

In naming these three cautions about worship, power, and community, I hope to spark reflection about how the Bible is used and read in your community. To contest biblical authoritarianism, we need to call out and interrogate ways the Bible is used to throw people under the bus and promote fear and hate rather than love and human flourishing across the globe.

Biblical Authoritarianism and Christian Nationalism's Hermeneutic of Hate

In seminary there's a buzzword that theologians and Bible professors frequently use. That buzzword is "hermeneutics." Hermeneutics is the discipline or science of interpretation. Hermeneutics focuses on questions of meaning and meaning making. For example, does meaning come from biblical authors, biblical texts, or readers of the Bible? Tricky question, right? As scholars have sought to answer this question, numerous methods of biblical interpretation have emerged as we aim to interpret ancient texts "responsibly" for our modern context. The danger of imposing our will on Scripture and manipulating the Bible

---

7. Parker, *If God Still Breathes*, 28.

to make it mean something it never meant is a real and present danger for all Christians.

In his provocatively titled book *Republican Jesus: How the Right Has Rewritten the Gospels*, Tony Keddie argues that, "When a modern community fixes the meaning of a biblical text as a basis for discrimination on the grounds of religion, race, ethnicity, sexuality, gender, class, citizenship, or ability, I view this as a hermeneutics of hate."[8] Keddie calls this a hermeneutic of hate because it imposes a particular way of interpreting the Bible to "classify certain individuals as inferior to others."[9] To achieve this hateful end, Keddie argues that right-wing influencers:

> *Garble* the text by mistranslating or limiting the meaning of its words . . . *Omit* relevant parts of the text by extracting a verse from its literary context and sometimes cutting out sections of verses . . . *Patch* this cut-up text together with other cut-up texts into the framework of a carefully designed quilt that's backed by ignorance, stuffed with hatred, and sewn with self-interest.[10]

Garble, omit, and patch—these are all ways of reading the Bible that lead to authoritarian readings of the Bible. These reading strategies are not hard to illustrate among Christian nationalists.

For example, in the city of Spokane Valley, where I grew up visiting my grandparents weekly, a local pastor named Matt Shea was elected to serve the Washington State House of Representatives as a Republican from 2009–2021. Shea's tenure as a state representative was riddled with controversies, including support for three acts of political violence, an armed road rage incident, and domestic abuse accusations by his first wife (who also claimed that Shea made her walk on his left side because his sword goes on his right side).[11]

8. Keddie, *Republican Jesus*, 8.

9. Keddie, *Republican Jesus*, 9.

10. All three points are from Keddie, *Republican Jesus*, 9–10, emphasis original.

11. See Craig, "Divorced Candidate." The three acts of political violence were the Bundy standoff in Nevada in 2014, an armed standoff in Priest River

In October of 2018 a manifesto written by Shea, titled, "Biblical Basis for War," was discovered that garbles, omits, and patches together verses of the Bible to justify war against America's tyrants, who Shea believes are any "godless leader" (a rather garbled understanding of tyranny to put it mildly). According to Shea's manifesto, the enemy must surrender on these terms: "1. Stop all abortions; 2. No same-sex marriage; 3. No idolatry or occultism; 4. No communism; and 5. Must obey Biblical law."[12] If they do not submit, Shea writes, "kill all males."

Shea's biblical manifesto brazenly embraces a hermeneutic of hate. Notably, of sixteen Bible verses quoted, only three come from the New Testament (the epistles of James and Hebrews) and Jesus is only mentioned once to appeal to "freedom in Christ." The problem is not that Shea is drawing on the Old Testament; the problem is that he conveniently draws on violent Old Testament texts while omitting hundreds of Old Testament texts on love, grace, peace, charity, hospitality, and critiques of pride.

Moreover, as Whitworth University professor James Edwards in Spokane argued in an interview about Shea's manifesto, "No war in the Bible was waged over abortion or same-sex marriage or communism."[13] This is the danger of a hermeneutic of hate: one can garble, omit, and patch biblical texts together to impose their violent fantasies onto Scripture. Lest one think that Shea's biblical manifesto is the product of being uneducated, he holds a bachelor's and law degree from Gonzaga University.

The real-life damage that a hermeneutic of hate can cause the vulnerable can also reach the highest levels of US government. For example, in 2018, after the Trump administration implemented a draconian policy to separate children from their families at the US-Mexico border, former Attorney General Jeff Sessions appealed to Rom 13:1–7 to call for blind passivity to the Trump

---

in 2015, and the right-wing takeover of the Malheur Wildlife Refuge in Oregon in 2016.

12. For transcript, see https://www.spokesman.com/documents/2018/oct/25/biblical-basis-war/.

13. See Criscione, "Spokane County Commission."

administration's family separation policy. Notably, Romans 13 is one of the most notoriously abused passages in the New Testament and appears to call for passive obedience to state power if one *omits* its larger epistolary context. I encourage you to grab a Bible and read Romans 12 through 14 if you need to jog your memory.

During a press conference, Sessions publicly embraced a hermeneutic of hate when he omitted the context of Romans 12 and 14 (not to mention the rest of the letter) in the following statement: "I would cite you to the Apostle Paul and his clear and wise command in Romans 13, to obey the laws of the government because God has ordained them for the purpose of order. Orderly and lawful processes are good in themselves and protect the weak and lawful."[14] For her part, White House Press Secretary Sarah Huckabee Sanders defended Sessions' comment at a press conference: "It is very biblical to enforce the law."[15] When Paul penned these words in the 50s CE before he was martyred by Roman power, did he really intend for them to invite blind submission to governing authorities who are separating children from their parents?

I will never forget the day that Sessions made his statement about Romans 13. As a Bible teacher, it hurt. I felt physically ill, especially as images of locked up children permeated the media. The cruelty took my breath away. Thankfully, I was not alone. The day after Sessions' comment, my friend and former colleague Michael Gorman posted a viral thread on Facebook that systematically rebuked Sessions' interpretation of Romans 13. Gorman is a world-renowned expert on Paul's letters and some of his points are worth quoting in full here as I can't say it any better. Here I only quote five of his nine points that are now published in his Romans commentary. Gorman argues:

1. Whatever Romans 13:1–7 means, it cannot be understood in a way that contradicts its context.

2. The immediate context of Romans 13:1–7 is the entirety of Romans 12 and 13. In Romans 12 and 13, Paul sets out basic

14. See Zauzumer and McMillan, "Sessions Cites Bible."
15. See Stewart, "Sarah Sanders on Immigrant Family."

guidelines for the Christian communities in Rome, and for us.

3. Those guidelines begin with a call for *nonconformity to this age*, a radical transformation of attitudes and practices that is appropriate to those who have benefited from God's mercy in Christ (Rom 12:1–2). This spirit of nonconformity and transformation is the prerequisite for knowing and doing God's will. And it is the fundamental framework for everything that follows, including 13:1–7.

4. In Romans 12:9–21, after a brief discussion of various gifts in the body of Christ, Paul calls on the Christian community to practice a radical, genuine form of love that corresponds to the love they have received from God in Christ. This includes hating what is evil and practicing the good; showing hospitality to strangers; loving enemies; weeping with those who weep; associating with the lowly; blessing persecutors; not repaying evil for evil; practicing peace toward all; not seeking vengeance for harm done; and overcoming evil with good. The call to this lifestyle is what immediately precedes Romans 13:1–7.

5. This context for Romans 13:1–7 means that the Christian community must not follow any authority or law that calls us to violate the basic Christian principles presented in the texts surrounding 13:1–7, because in so doing we would be failing to "put on the Lord Jesus Christ" (Rom 13:14). Rather than being a blanket call to obedience and allegiance, which is reserved for God alone, Romans 13:1–7—when read in context—actually supports Christian opposition to many laws and practices. *The Christian is free from the tyranny of obedience to political figures and entities but obligated to love and to work for the common good, even when doing so is an act of disobedience.*[16]

---

16. See Gorman, *Romans*, 258–59.

Dr. Gorman offers a powerful example of what it can look like to confront biblical authoritarianism in public. One way to continue this work is to offer the watching world new reading strategies that interpret the Bible *literarily* rather than ones that garble, omit, and patch the Bible together to read select passages *literally*. As I always tell my students, one of the most important things you can learn in seminary is to never, ever build an entire theology or ethic based on one passage of the Bible.

While Shea's and Sessions' approach to the Bible may seem extreme, recent Pew Research Center data shows just how widespread biblical authoritarianism is in the United States. Among those who want the US to be a Christian nation, over 50 percent believe that the Bible should influence US law and, when they conflict, take precedence over the will of the people.[17] This number goes up to 65 percent among white evangelicals. Biblical authoritarianism is not compatible with democratic values. In a moment when the Bible and its interpreters are rightly under much scrutiny, there is a temptation to throw the Bible out with the bathwater. I believe the Bible still matters profoundly for this moment. To disorient authoritarian and coercive hermeneutics of hate, we need a better and more life-giving way of reading the Bible.

Toward a "Public" and Christocentric Hermeneutic of Love and Resistance

A recent interview with one of America's most learned historians on race and religion in the United States hit me like a ton of bricks. The interview was with Professor David Hollinger, who was being asked about Christianity's role on the political left and right and Christian nationalism's threat to democracy. At the end of the interview, Hollinger argues that progressive ecumenical Christians "have been relatively silent in public about how deficient they find evangelical views of the Bible." As a result, Hollinger argues that progressive Christians "have yielded to evangelicals much of the

17. See Smith et al., "45% of Americans."

symbolic capital of Christianity." Hollinger then asks, can progressives "reclaim the Bible?" He answers, "Perhaps. But to do that, you have to actually make arguments, and in public."[18] Zing!

To challenge Christian nationalism, we have to make *public* arguments about the Bible. The answer for challenging biblical authoritarianism in this moment is more Bible—not less. I anticipate that this will make some Christians challenging Christian nationalism uncomfortable. If that's you, I get it, but I also want to say this: It's okay to name the harm the Bible and its interpreters have caused while simultaneously interpreting the Bible for the common good—to bring peace, justice, and salvation to all flesh. We can do both and we can do them responsibly and well. You don't have to rescue the Bible from itself to be a faithful Christian. To make good public arguments about the Bible, we need an interpretive handrail that leads us toward love and strategic nonviolence rather than fear and coercive hate. One interpretive handrail that can guide us in the right direction is what I'm calling a Christocentric hermeneutic of love and resistance.

Before moving to Anabaptist Mennonite Biblical Seminary, I taught at a historic Roman Catholic seminary called St. Mary's Seminary and University in Baltimore, Maryland. It was an incredible experience that profoundly shaped my vocation as a Bible teacher. Most of my courses at St. Mary's were at a night school called the Ecumenical Institute of Theology, where I routinely had diverse students from across the political and theological spectrum. Sometimes I even had a few ambassadors and accommodators of Christian nationalism sitting next to resisters and rejecters.

Amidst this vast difference, I was struck that I could get ambassadors and accommodators to track with my critique of neoliberalism, white supremacy, mass incarceration, and structural racism as long as I stayed close to the whole life of Jesus in its ancient context. But the second I shifted from what the text *meant* to what I think it *means* today, I immediately lost my ambassador and accommodator students, who argued that my interpretation was a socialist, liberal, or Democrat reading. On the one hand, this

18. See Steinmetz-Jenkins, "Christianity's Place in the Left and the Right."

experience reminded me just how clouded some of these students' interpretive lenses are by partisan loyalties. On the other hand, it gave me hope that staying close to the biblical text—especially the whole life of Jesus—can nurture shifts of loyalty.

The interpretive lens through which many Christian nationalists read Scripture is tinted with red, white, and blue, and is anchored in loyalty to one's ethnic and partisan identity. I call this a state-centric hermeneutic. To challenge a state-centric hermeneutic, we need an altogether different lens through which to read Scripture and anchor to which to cleave. I believe that lens and anchor is Jesus Christ. In theology, we call this a "Christ-centered," or Christocentric hermeneutic. A Christocentric hermeneutic is a way of reading the Bible through a Jesus-centered lens rather than a state-centered, fear-centered, or a me-centered lens. It is an attempt to read Scripture the way Jesus read Scripture because, at the end of the day, we worship Jesus and not the Bible itself.

For Jesus, a Christocentric hermeneutic meant reading himself into the biblical story as the fulfillment of God's promises to Israel. Take, for example, Jesus' famous inaugural sermon in his hometown synagogue at Nazareth, where he quotes the Jewish Scriptures to announce good news for the poor, release for prisoners, recovery of sight for the blind, and freedom for the oppressed (Luke 4:16–21). Strikingly, after Jesus quotes the Old Testament, his only original words are, "Today this Scripture is fulfilled in your ears" (Luke 4:21). For Jesus, the good news of forgiveness and debt release in the Old Testament Scriptures points to himself, not tomorrow or next week, but *today*!

Jesus' Christocentric hermeneutic is also felt after Jesus is raised from the dead and meets two confused disciples on the road to Emmaus. To correct their confusion, Luke writes that Jesus began with "Moses and all the prophets" and "he interpreted to them the things about himself in all the scriptures" (Luke 24:27). Jesus' reliance on the law of Moses and the prophets is a reminder of just how *Jewish* the early Jesus movement was. It is also a trenchant reminder that, in the words of Amy-Jill Levine, "You don't need to make Judaism look bad in order to make Jesus and Paul look good."[19] The Jewish Jesus rooted in the Scriptures of Israel gives us tools to challenge strange worship and a hermeneutic of hate. Moreover, in magnifying the life of Jesus as our final authority, the Bible is "removed from the vulnerable position of encouraging an 'idolatry of the book.'"[20] Here my aim is not to minimize the authority and sacredness of the Bible but rather to maximize the authority of the life and teachings of Jesus for making sense of and taking Scripture seriously in the way that Jesus took Scripture seriously.

At the heart of Jesus' Christocentric hermeneutic is also an emphasis on "resistance." I don't use this word lightly. The word "resistance" has all sorts of cultural baggage, especially since so many American pundits conflate "resistance" with "violent resistance" or certain leftist movements (for example, the nonviolent resistance of Black Lives Matter with the violent resistance of Antifa). This is unfortunate. To be a Christian is to live a life of resistance every day against sin, temptation, and anti-God forces in this world. We need to de-stigmatize the word "resistance" because to be a Christian is to participate in acts of everyday resistance that defy the allure and power of strange worship.

Resistance, at its core, is any public action that attempts to undermine power. Resistance can use direct violence; it can also use strategic nonviolence and noncompliance. Scholars of resistance movements observe that resistance has a compounding effect: resistance often inspires more resistance. Because of this compounding effect, a hermeneutic of resistance sees biblical interpretation as a site of direct action and strategic nonviolence that generates social transformation *and* participation in the work of change-making.

To invite participation, a hermeneutic of resistance leverages narratives of resistance in the ancient world to analogously challenge strange worship in today's world. It offers a confrontative alternative to theologies of oppression and is thereby intimately bound up with biblical notions of repentance as changing one's

19. See Levine, "Alumni Profiles."
20. Smith, *Bible Made Impossible,* 124.

mind about who God is, how God is at work in the world, power, and racism. A hermeneutic of resistance is a call to public biblical interpretation. It is an invitation to mobilize congregations in the struggle to dismantle idols that distort our knowledge of God and neighbor. A hermeneutic of resistance interrogates power, discerns effective resistance, and, ultimately, finds expression in congregational movements that publicly interrupt power worship.

But to paraphrase the apostle Paul, if I have a Christocentric hermeneutic of resistance, so as to challenge Christian nationalism, but do not have love, I am nothing (1 Cor 13:1ff). Without love, any attempt to challenge Christian nationalism through biblical interpretation may err on the side of doing more harm than good. In her brilliantly titled book *Even the Devil Quotes Scripture*, New Testament scholar Robyn Whitaker calls for a "hermeneutic of love" in contrast to literal readings of the Bible that lead to a hermeneutic of hate. Whitaker observes that the Old Testament verse most quoted in the New Testament is Leviticus 19:18: "you shall love your neighbor as yourself."[21] Almost every author of the New Testament quotes this verse, often alongside the double love command to love God *and* neighbor (Matt 22:35–40; Mark 12:28–34; Luke 10:27). Notably, Paul even argues that "love is the fulfilling of the law" (Rom 13:9).

The love command offers a powerful paradigm for reading the Bible responsibly today—one that finds deep resonance with how the authors of the New Testament read and used Scripture. Whitaker suggests that a hermeneutic of love is best posed as a question: "Does this interpretation lead to more love of God and neighbor?"[22] That is a question we all need to ask as a handrail and guiding north star as we navigate the polarized and contested waters of public biblical interpretation.

To get in the way of strange worship, we need more Bible and not less. A Christocentric hermeneutic of love and resistance is one way we can participate in making public arguments about the Bible for the common good.

21. Whitaker, *Even the Devil Quotes Scripture*, 129.

22. Whitaker, *Even the Devil Quotes Scripture*, 144.

Is Christian Nationalism a Form of Violent Extremism?

I was recently lecturing on white Christian nationalism to a group of mostly Muslim PhD students who are studying approaches to countering violent extremism. At the end of my lecture, a student from Pakistan asked, "Do you think Christian nationalism in the United State is a form of violent extremism?" The question made me pause.

On the one hand, if we reduce our definition of violent extremism to direct violence (war, murder, terrorism) then the answer is that sometimes Christian nationalism is a form of violent extremism. But if we expand the definition to include structural violence (the normalization of oppressive hierarchies) and cultural violence (racism, homophobia, and misogyny), then the answer is that white Christian nationalism is unequivocally a form of violent extremism. To this, we can add that Christian nationalism is a form of violent extremism because it dehumanizes other groups, rejects democratic methods of change, and condones violence to create a "pure" society.[23]

Hindsight is always 20/20, but here's what I wish I said to that PhD student: I believe that white Christian nationalism is a form of violent extremism because it provides the theological and ideological justification for normalizing structural, cultural, and symbolic violence in the United States. Taking a minute to define these terms about violence will bring this point into sharper focus.

The twentieth century is known as the "age of murder." No less than 170 million humans lost their lives to direct violence—mostly at the hands of state power. The repetitive pattern of direct violence can be traced back through every generation of human existence. What stands out about the twentieth century is the development of technologies to orchestrate mass killings more effectively. Two World Wars and the Holocaust culminated in the United States inventing and dropping a nuclear bomb on Hiroshima and Nagasaki,

---

23. On these points and more, I encourage my readers to make the following free PDF resource available to their congregations: Schirch, "Making Peace in a Violent World."

Japan. In the blink of an eye, an estimated 180–200 thousand innocent civilians lost their lives.[24] What was intended to stop evil perpetuated more of it, including a nuclear arms race that remains one of the greatest threats to human existence and world peace.

If we reduce our understanding of violence to physical violence in the twentieth century, we will miss the ways non-physical or, at least, less-physical forms of violence impact everyday life. Violence in everyday life is multidimensional and sneaky; it is *structural, cultural,* and *symbolic.* Structural violence normalizes oppressive systems without necessarily inflicting death. Structural violence forms dehumanizing social hierarchies across weaponized lines of human difference such as class, race, gender, age, sexuality, and ethnicity. It is encrusted in our systems of finance, law, education, politics, health, food, clean water, transportation, housing, interpersonal relationships, and even houses of worship. It is still defined as violence because it brings about harm, creating the conditions for the systemic flourishing of some while minimizing or denying that same flourishing to others. Fueled by the interests of the dominant culture, it fabricates social stigmas to organize power around the privileged and undermine power around the underprivileged. There's a reason why the north shore of Chicago is predominantly white and rich, and the south side Black and under-resourced. Structural violence doesn't always kill but it always dehumanizes, segregates, and impoverishes.

The sneakiness of structural violence is that those who benefit from it either deny it exists or don't see that it exists at all. Structural violence is oppression camouflaged as the way things just are in one's culture. This leads to cultural violence, which is a worldview and language of power that sanctions direct *and* structural violence against the marginalized. Here in the United States, the legacy of enslaving Africans to build a nation with free labor cast a long shadow of cultural violence fueled by white supremacy. White supremacy is cultural violence. It *legitimizes* the exploitation of Black bodies through an artificial racial caste system that

24. See www.atomicarchive.com/resources/documents/med/med_chp10.html.

is policed through structures (law, segregation, armed police) and direct violence (lynching, police brutality, mass incarceration).

As Isabel Wilkerson writes of the Jim Crow era, "The dominant caste devised a labyrinth of laws to hold the newly freed people on the bottom rung ever more tightly . . . People on the bottom rung could be beaten or killed with impunity for any breach of the caste system, like not stepping off the sidewalk fast enough or trying to vote."[25] The cycle is vicious: cultural violence can lead to death, but it can also create the conditions for long-term poverty and marginalization, stimulating what Johan Galtung calls a "silent holocaust" that slowly erodes a community's well-being.[26]

Violence, then, is direct, structural, and cultural—but it is also symbolic. Symbolic violence is non-physical violence that lurks in the shadows of our social relations. Symbolic violence *normalizes* the imagined underdogs' subordinate place in one's culture. So, women are inferior to men (patriarchy). Wealthy businessmen just work harder than the so-called poor (capitalism). America is more blessed and powerful than Mexico (ethnocentrism). Black bodies are inherently more violent than white bodies (racism). Immigrants increase crime (xenophobia). Taken together, these egregious social stigmas create power imbalances that normalize oppressive relationships. This can lead to direct violence against the imagined underdog, including sexualized violence and cultural marginalization.

What students and scholars of violent extremism have taught me is that violent extremism can be challenged, especially since people don't radicalize overnight. As I discussed in chapter 4, radicalization takes about five years from exposure to radical ideas to acts of harm. One way to disrupt this radicalization process is to engage what peace studies scholars call "counternarratives."

25. Wilkerson, *Caste*, 48.
26. Galtung, "Twenty-Five Years of Peace Research," 146–47.

Preaching the Whole Life of Jesus as Counternarrative

I believe that preaching and teaching the whole life of Jesus is our most effective tool for challenging Christian nationalism's violent extremism. As one scholar of violent extremism argues, "narratives are often used by extremist groups to seed resentment, disconnection, and violence in order to gain sympathy and draw in new members."[27] The power of narratives to indoctrinate and radicalize willing listeners has led some scholars of violent extremism to no longer talk about "radicalization" and, instead, to talk about "recruitment." Narratives have the power to recruit and counter-recruit.

Christian nationalists are especially susceptible to recruitment by narratives of resentment and fear because the gospel of MAGA Jesus includes personal salvation in Jesus but excludes salvation through the whole life of Jesus. This includes Jesus' resurrection and teachings on power, violence, peace, inclusive table fellowship, and following Jesus' clear summary of the law as loving God *and* neighbor.

The gospel of MAGA Jesus is not hard to illustrate. Its foothold on congregations, home school curricula, and youth and children's ministries is felt across the United States and abroad. It can even be found in children's Bibles. For example, pastor Robert Jeffress, who was one of Trump's first and most outspoken evangelical advocates, has a children's Bible that is marketed to his 13,000-member First Baptist Church in Dallas, Texas, along with his radio program on over 800 stations and television programs that purportedly reach 195 countries. Instead of beginning the gospel story with creation or God's love, Jeffress begins the gospel story with judgment to remind kids that some people "go to hell, where the devil lives, and they suffer . . . It's a permanent time-out." He then likens God's punishment for sin as "far worse than a spanking" and argues that Jesus took this spanking for us by dying on a cross. [28]

27. Slachmuijlder, "Peacebuilding Narratives," 284.

28. Jeffress, "Gift," 3, 9.

Jeffress' story of the gospel is much closer to a fire insurance policy that forgives sin than the gospel of the New Testament. Most strikingly, Jeffress omits the resurrection, which is the heartbeat of the gospel in the New Testament in summaries of the gospel (1 Cor 15:1–8; Phil 2:6–11; 2 Tim 2:8), gospel sermons (see throughout Acts), and biographies of the gospel (Matthew, Mark, Luke, John). Jeffress' gospel is incomplete—it recruits disciples into eternal salvation, but not into the resurrection-powered *way of Jesus for the life of this world*. For certain, he goes out of his way to make sure children know that doing good things like feeding the poor, sharing possessions, and helping others have no bearing on one's standing before God.

Jeffress' gospel for children might seem like low hanging fruit. It's not. I used to preach a similar gospel as a Young Life leader to hundreds of teenagers. The gospel I preached was obsessed with three things: sin, Jesus' death, and one's personal relationship with Jesus. Sometimes I even found myself preaching this gospel to strangers in coffee shops to save them from hell. My gospel had little need for the church or the social teachings of Jesus. It wasn't until my friend and academic mentor Scot McKnight wrote a book on the gospel that my own gospel's shortcomings came into stark focus. McKnight's argument is simple. He argues that Jesus didn't preach personal salvation or Paul's doctrine of justification for the forgiveness of sins.[29] Rather, he proclaimed himself as the arrival of God's saving reign and rule called the kingdom of God. This idea changed my life.

As I now always tell my students, if we get the kingdom wrong, we are going to get the life and teachings of Jesus wrong. The kingdom of God was the centering message of Jesus' life and ministry. Jesus' gospel message was something bigger and more all-encompassing than personal salvation. It was an invitation to Israel and the gentile world to reorient life around a different kind of king—to become active participants in God's inbreaking kingdom of peace, justice, reparation, forgiveness, and debt release.

29. McKnight, *King Jesus Gospel.*

The perennial danger for all Christians is the temptation to conflate the kingdom of God with the militarized kingdoms of this world. This temptation is especially felt among ambassadors and accommodators of Christian nationalism. For example, in a fiery speech at a Colorado church, congresswoman Lauren Boebert argued, "The church is supposed to direct the government. The government is not supposed to direct the church."[30] Boebert's dominionist vision falls flat when placed alongside the life of Jesus. For example, when Jesus is tempted by Satan in the wilderness, Satan offers Jesus authority over all the kingdoms of this world, claiming "it has been given over to me, and I give it to anyone I please" (Luke 4:6).

The passage implies (with a subtle critique of Rome) that the kingdoms of this world lie under the authority of Satan. Jesus repudiates this offer of political power by recognizing that it is a test to see if he will break the boundaries of the political metaphor of idolatry. Jesus repudiates Satan's offer of power by quoting the first commandment: "Worship the Lord your God, and serve only him" (Luke 4:8). For Jesus, the seduction of "God and country" nationalism is incompatible with loyalty to and proclamation of God's coming kingdom. This kingdom, in fact, does not arrive through military might and cultural violence. Rather, it arrives through a new covenant of peace inaugurated through Jesus' death and resurrection (Luke 22:14–23; 1 Cor 11:23–26). This is why Jesus' resurrection was so important for early Christian preaching—it signaled to the world "that the *mode* of Jesus' salvation has been vindicated by God as the way of true salvation, and the violent modes of ethnic cleansing, imperial domination, and the like are pseudo-soteriologies [or false forms of salvation]."[31]

A biblical emphasis on preaching the whole life of Jesus is especially evident in one of the most well-known passages in Matthew's Gospel called the Great Commission. The Great Commission is a key prooftext for Christian dominionist thought-leaders, who love the part where Jesus claims to "have all authority in

30. See Sulliman and Bella, "GOP Rep. Boebert."
31. Gorman, *Inhabiting the Cruciform God,* 139.

heaven and on earth . . . therefore go make disciples of all nations" (Matt 28:19–19), but they garble and omit verse 20, which says: "and telling them to obey everything I have commanded you."[32] This means teaching disciples to obey Jesus' teachings on power, boundaries, and order, including inclusive table fellowship with marginalized persons. It also means teaching about Jesus' teachings on wealth ethics, violence, and active peacemaking in the Sermon on the Mount. Jesus incarnated these ethical teachings as a sign and foretaste of the arrival of the kingdom of God. When disciples of Jesus do the same, we become active participants in God's reconciling mission to bring peace and justice to earth, or what the New Testament calls a "new heaven and a new earth" (Rev 21:1; 2 Pet 3:13).

Notwithstanding Jesus' clear command, Christians have gone out of their way to explain away the ethical demands of the kingdom of God. The Sermon on the Mount's history of interpretation brings this point into focus. For some, the Sermon on the Mount is just an inward, spiritual disposition. For others, the Sermon on the Mount is only meant to be lived out by clergy. For some, it is an impossible ideal. For others, it is an interim ethic for a failed Jewish Messiah. For some, it is a template of heaven for the afterlife— and not life in this world. More recently, according to evangelical leader Russell Moore, the ethical demands of Jesus are understood by congregants as "liberal talking points." Moore goes on to say that "what was alarming to me is that in most of these scenarios, when the pastor would say, 'I'm literally quoting Jesus Christ,' the response would not be, 'I apologize.' The response would be, 'Yes, but that doesn't work anymore. That's weak.'"[33]

When the church emphasizes personal salvation at the expense of Jesus' whole saving life, we create disciples who misinterpret the way of Jesus as weakness and as liberal talking points. This

---

32. For example, see Torba and Isker's frequent appeal to the Great Commission in *Christian Nationalism*. They write, "Jesus did not command us to sit around getting crushed by Satan waiting to die. He commanded us to make disciples of all nations and we need to take dominion in His name" (5).

33. See Reed, "Pastor Alarmed."

is strange worship. The ethics of God's in-breaking kingdom are not liberal talking points. They are badges of covenantal membership for citizens and emissaries of God's kingdom. Yes, salvation is by grace, but living out Jesus' commandments are how we *participate* in and bear *witness* to God's grace extended to us.

One of the most exciting contributions to New Testament studies in recent memory is a book on grace by the formidable New Testament scholar John M. G. Barclay. Barclay likens the Western church's understanding of grace to our relationship with Santa Claus. Santa makes a list of who is naughty and nice and delivers gifts accordingly. Santa's gifts are "conditioned" and given only to worthy individuals with no obligation to do anything in return. Grace in the New Testament, in contrast, is given to unworthy recipients and "is free (unconditioned) but not cheap (without expectation or obligation). Those who have received it are to remain within it, their lives altered by new habits, new dispositions, and new practices of grace."[34] These new habits and practices of grace look like Jesus, who is the grace of God incarnate.

When we teach and preach the whole life of Jesus we throw strange worship off-kilter. If you ever find yourself forgetting what the whole gospel is, just think of the Gospel according to Matthew, Mark, Luke, and John. The early church intentionally named these biographies of Jesus "Gospels" because when we preach Jesus, we preach the good news of the gospel. The whole gospel of Jesus Christ is our counternarrative against MAGA Jesus and his influencers. Counternarratives create spaces for counter-recruitment against cultural rip tides that draw people toward the harmful currents of violent extremism. Jesus is our counternarrative and the church is where we do counter-recruitment by telling the whole gospel.

34. Barclay, *Paul and the Power of Grace*, 149.

The Way of Jesus and the Spiral of Violence

In his book *Disarming the Church,* Eric Seibert argues that Christians tend to look the other way from violence because (1) we believe violence stops evil and saves lives; (2) we have been desensitized to the horror of violence; (3) we are unaware of viable alternatives to violence; (4) we do not believe nonviolence will work in certain situations; (5) we misapply sacred texts that sanction violence; (6) we rarely hear the church call us to love enemies and live nonviolently; (7) we receive mixed messages about violence from the church; and (8) we confuse the demands of the state with the will of God.[35]

Each of Seibert's points deserve serious reflection as we imagine how to challenge Christian nationalism's violent extremism with the way of Jesus. But point 8, when Christians confuse the demands of the state with the will of God, represents a particularly significant stumbling block for challenging Christian nationalism.

In his now well-known work on ethnic conflict and violence, theologian Miroslav Volf attributes Christians' incompetence and paralysis in the face of violent conflict to "idolatrous shifts of loyalty." Volf suggests that such idolatrous loyalties create Christians who give "ultimate allegiance to the gospel of Jesus Christ" but "in fact seem to have an overriding commitment to their respective culture, ethnic group, or nation. In conflict situations, they tend to fight on the side of their group and are tempted to employ faith as a weapon in the struggle."[36]

As I discussed at length in chapter 4, this is why Christian nationalism is a form of strange worship. It is a worldview that pledges loyalty to one's ethno-racial identity in the face of conflict, even if that means lording one's faith over and against one's neighbor. Philip Gorski and Samuel Perry capture this dynamic well in their definition of Christian nationalism as a "desire to restore and privilege the myths, values, identity, and authority of a particular ethnocultural tribe. These beliefs add up to a political

35. Seibert, *Disarming the Church,* 32–45.
36. Volf, "Social Meaning of Reconciliation," 159.

vision that privileges that tribe. And they seek to put other tribes in their 'proper' place."[37] To challenge this "us" vs. "them" narrative, we need to talk more about Jesus' and Paul's attitude toward violent extremism.

One of the most shocking things I learned about Jesus in seminary was that Jesus' proclamation of the kingdom of God matters for how we think about our neighbors, enmity, and violent conflict in this world. Up until this point in my life, evangelicalism taught me well that Jesus reconciled me to God, but it failed to teach me about Christ's invitation to participate in a "ministry of reconciliation" with others in this world (2 Cor 5:18). It's true that Jesus proclaimed that "his kingdom is not of this world" (John 18:36), but this does not mean that his kingdom is not a presence and "sphere of interruptive nonviolence" *within this world*.[38]

The apostle Paul certainly resonates with this thinking. After all, Paul converted from a violent extremist (Gal 1:13, 23; Phil 3:6; 1 Cor 15:9) to a nonviolent peacemaker when he experienced an "apocalypse/revelation of Jesus Christ" (Gal 1:12). In response to Paul's revelation of Christ, Paul became the theological architect of gentile inclusion into God's family. To describe and imagine this global community, Paul uses the Greek word for "peace" (*eirēnē*) forty-four times in his letters, along with its cognates "to live in peace" (*eirēneuō*) three times and "to make peace" (*eirēnopoieō*) one time.[39] Strikingly, Paul only uses the word *eirēnē* to signify peace between humans and God one time in his letters (Rom 5:1). The forty-three other occurrences of *eirēnē* occur in contexts that talk about the "God of peace" and social, cosmic, political, ecclesial, and inner-spiritual realities.[40] For Paul, social dimensions of God's in-breaking peace through the kingdom of God matter for human relationships. Indeed, Paul's conversion to Jesus' way of

---

37. Gorski and Perry, *Flag and the Cross,* 14.

38. Wengst, *Pax Romana and the Peace of Jesus Christ*, 88.

39. See Strait, "Idols, Idolatry."

40. When discussing vertical dimensions of soteriology, Paul prefers the reconciliation word family (Rom 5:10–11; 2 Cor 5:18–20; Eph 2:16; Col 1:20, 22).

peace offers a powerful counternarrative to violent extremists who perpetuate, rather than interrupt, cycles of violence.

Hélder Câmara, a Brazilian Catholic archbishop and liberation theologian, called this cruel cycle the "spiral of violence."[41] The spiral of violence, according to Câmara, manifests in three forms: Violence No. 1, where the privileged oppress the underdog; Violence No. 2, where the oppressed underdog retaliates with violence; and Violence No. 3, where the privileged preserve their power by responding with overwhelming violent repression. In Câmara's own words, "Violence attracts violence."[42] The attraction is a magnetic and death-dealing force. Violence begets violence. Violence + violent retaliation = more violence. Shooting your enemy means his or her friends might shoot back. Violence is a cyclical diseased social imagination in need of repair. What is the solution?

The life of Jesus is God's revolution against the spiral of violence (as Paul's transformation from a violent extremist suggests). This revolution was not led by armed insurgents. It was led by God's unarmed human one, Jesus of Nazareth, who claimed that the kingdom was drawing near. The nearness of this kingdom stood in stark contrast to the palpable nearness of Rome's military occupation of Jesus' home country. Under the guise of "peace," Rome pacified (or, "peace-ified") distant peoples, including Israel, through military domination (direct violence), taxation (structural violence), enslavement (cultural violence), and racialized stigmas (symbolic violence). Together, the empire called these mechanisms of violent domination the "Roman peace" (in Latin, the *pax Romana*). The propaganda of the Roman peace, however, referred to peace through *coercion*. Rome's peace-ification of subordinate peoples is best exemplified in Roman crucifixion, a torture apparatus used to *make* subjects peaceful.

41. Câmara, *Spiral of Violence*, 25–36. On Câmara's influence, see Cramer and Werntz, *Field Guide to Christian Nonviolence*, 117–21. I'm grateful to *Made for Pax* for permission to republish part of my essay, "The Myth of Redemptive Violence" in this section.

42. Câmara, *Spiral of Violence*, 30.

Jesus was not the first Jew to resist Rome's manufactured peace through coercion. Jewish messianic pretenders, armed guerilla warriors, and prophetic movements sought to overthrow Rome with Violence No. 2. Rome's overwhelming military strength easily suppressed these resistance movements, culminating in Rome's destruction of the Jerusalem Temple in 70 CE through Violence No. 3. Violence begot violence. It is into this vicious spiral of violence that Jesus injected his own life and teachings by drawing on the wisdom and strategic nonviolence of Jewish sages and prophets. At every point of Jesus' public ministry, we witness God incarnate calling into existence a people who will interrupt peace through coercion with radical acts of neighborly love and nonviolent resistance.

> In teaching to turn the other check, Jesus shamed Violence No. 1.
>
> In teaching enemy love, Jesus disrupted Violence No. 2.
>
> In teaching the things that make for peace, Jesus stymied Violence No. 3.
>
> In proclaiming freedom for prisoners, Jesus interrupted structural violence.
>
> In practicing inclusive table fellowship, Jesus flustered cultural violence.
>
> In including women among his disciples, Jesus disoriented symbolic violence.
>
> In proclaiming good news to the poor, Jesus undermined economic caste systems.
>
> In eating with tax collectors, Jesus practiced enemy love.
>
> In speaking woes to the rich, Jesus condemned hoarding wealth.
>
> In blessing peacemakers, Jesus contested the efficacy of violent resistance.
>
> In healing the diseased, Jesus showed the limitations of state and military power.
>
> In forgiving sins, Jesus redefined power.

In publicly dying on a Roman cross, Jesus exposed the spiral of violence.

In rising from the dead, Jesus publicly disarmed and made a public spectacle of the *pax Romana*.

Far from a call to *passivity*, the way of Jesus is a call to direct *action* and creative nonviolent *resistance*. It is an invitation to proclaim boldly and publicly that "peace is through Jesus Christ" (Acts 10:36). As Martin Luther King Jr. recalls, "True non-violent resistance is not unrealistic submission to evil power. It is rather a courageous confrontation of evil by the power of love, in the faith that it is better to be the recipient of violence than the inflictor of it, since the latter only multiplies the existence of violence and bitterness in the universe, while the former may develop a sense of shame in the opponent, and thereby bring about a transformation and change of heart."[43]

The first three centuries of early Christianity followed Jesus' way of peace. For Jesus and Paul, peace is more than inner tranquility. Peace is this, but it is so much more, including the transformation of violent extremists from inflictors of violence to interrupters of it.

Reclaiming the Bible as a Literature of Resistance

For two groups that hate each other so much, it is amazing how much Al-Qaeda and white Christian nationalism have in common. For example, both groups subscribe to a radical apocalyptic worldview that claims authoritarian readings of sacred texts, both believe that the end of times are upon us, both demonize their perceived enemies, and both believe that violence is redemptive.[44]

These are the character traits of radical apocalypticism. At the core of radical apocalypticism is the belief that the world is divided into good versus evil and that society is on the brink. This

43. Quoted in Washington, ed., *I Have a Dream*, 44.

44. See Flannery, "Radical Islamist and Radical Christianist Nuclear Terrorism," 83–84.

is why Donald Trump's apocalyptic language—"our country is going to hell!"—is so effective at whipping Christian nationalists into an "us" vs. "them" frenzy. To challenge white Christian nationalism, we need to think creatively about how to challenge radical apocalypticism.

Philip Gorski observes that radical apocalypticism is dangerous because it leads to arrogance (only followers know the truth), it demonizes enemies, and it leads to fatalism (which is the idea that wars and calamities are beyond human control).[45] Each of these dangers are present in a recent speech by conspiracy theorist Mike Lindell, who put on a summit to contest election integrity in the United States. While promoting Trump's Big Lie, Lindell pivots to boast that "there's a bright side, hey if we're wrong, it's End Times and all of us believers go up to Heaven. It's a win-win."[46]

Lindell's escapist theology has deep roots in American evangelicalism's publishing industrial complex about the end of times.[47] American evangelicals' obsession with the end of times has created a radical apocalyptic foundation for Christian nationalism that is not built on sand. For example, I will never forget hearing about Tim LaHaye and Jerry Jenkins's *Left Behind* novels when I was in high school. I didn't read them, but I remember teachers in my public school raving about the novels and friends consuming them like a Christian *Harry Potter* series as they all became fixated on how not to be left behind by Jesus.

At the heart of *Left Behind* is a radical apocalyptic worldview and a hermeneutic of hate against Catholics, LGBTQ+ persons, the United Nations, environmentalists, ecumenism, and peacemakers. Problematically, the authors reduce the gospel to fear of violent judgement and eternal damnation, wherein the faithful are "raptured" with Jesus and sinners are "left behind" to experience suffering on this earth. Even though the word rapture doesn't occur in the Bible, LaHaye and Jenkins garble the text to build an entire rapture theology off Paul's belief that believers will be

45. Gorski, *American Covenant,* 22.
46. See https://twitter.com/jimstewartson/status/1691831978767823270.
47. For a recent overview, see Hummel, *Rise and Fall of Dispensationalism.*

"caught up" in the clouds when Christ returns (1 Thess 4:17). The series has now sold over 60 million copies since 1995 and I have personally felt its impact among pastors and leaders in Africa and Latin America.

The *Left Behind* series patches together a violent fantasy of the end of times mostly based on the book of Revelation. Revelation is one of the most abused books of the Bible. Its otherworldly imagery and symbols are easy to garble into the service of hate. To read Revelation responsibly, we need to understand a thing or two about Jewish apocalyptic literature.

The word "apocalypse" comes from the Greek verb *apokalúptō* (which means to "reveal" or "uncover"). Apocalyptic is a genre of revelatory literature. Jewish apocalyptic literature emerged in the 160s BCE in response to a Hellenistic warrior king named Antiochus the IV who sought to violently erase Jewish identity by burning copies of Torah, desecrating the temple, and forcing Jewish mothers to not have their sons circumcised. During this time of trauma, apocalyptic visionaries like Daniel wrote apocalypses to empower Jews to remain faithful during persecution. In this sense, Jewish apocalyptic was a kind of crisis literature to "reveal" unseen realities about God's control over history when it seemed as if God had lost control. In this way, Jewish apocalyptic is a literature of resistance. Apocalyptic literature's bizarre imagery, symbols, and many-headed beasts are intentionally difficult for oppressors to understand. For insiders, however, apocalypses evoked theological imagination and, in the words of Revelation, "patient endurance" amidst suffering (Rev 1:9; 2:2, 3, 19; 3:10; 13:10; 14:12).

It is common knowledge among New Testament scholars today that Revelation includes the most sustained critique of Roman power in the New Testament. There is no small amount of irony in this, as Christian nationalists have sought to hijack its message to support American imperialism and the demonization of political enemies. More so, Revelation is not merely a book about the end of times. Rather, as Michael Gorman writes, "To read Revelation responsibly . . . is to read it not as a script for the future but as a script for the church."[48] In the first century context, this meant understanding the beast named 666 as code for spelling "Neron Caesar" (and not Obama or whoever one's latest anti-Christ is). John was writing to the church in the present tense and not strictly in the future tense, a form of exhortation that Anathea Portier-Young calls "apocalyptic preaching."

Apocalyptic preaching is a form of Christian public witness against political idolatry and injustice. It is a kind of apocalyptic resistance for the present moment. In this sense, apocalyptic is "Not a flight from reality. Not fear-mongering, labeling, or proclaiming 'the end is near.'"[49] Rather, apocalyptic preaching offers critique, exhortation, and consolation in the here and now for Christians living under the stressors, injustice, and allure of power worship and strange worship. Like John—and Jesus and Paul before him—the apocalyptic preacher "must do some hard diagnostic homework: What's going on in this community? In what are we deceived? How are we invested in the imperial project, and what does that cost us?"[50] This kind of diagnostic homework is crucial for pastors and leaders challenging white Christian nationalism's radical apocalypticism through critique, exhortation, and consolation.

Apocalyptic preaching also offers us a space for reclaiming the Bible as a literature of resistance against power worship. Through critique and exhortation, we can "unveil" the toxicity of biblical authoritarianism and the deception of MAGA Jesus. We can also challenge radical apocalypticism by reminding our communities that only God is in control of the end of times, that hate speech and racism are not the way of Jesus, that simple binaries between good versus evil rarely capture reality and, finally, that redemptive violence is a myth.[51]

---

48. See Gorman, *Reading Revelation Responsibly,* 189.

49. Portier-Young, "Apocalyptic Preaching."

50. Portier-Young, "Apocalyptic Preaching."

51. For these four points I lean on Flannery, "Radical Islamist and Radical Christianist Nuclear Terrorism," 86.

Vacation Bible School for Adults

I said a lot in this chapter, but really there's one thing I hope I communicated clearly: *The Bible matters for challenging white Christian nationalism.* In a moment when the Bible and its interpreters are rightly under much scrutiny, there is a temptation to push biblical interpretation aside and challenge white Christian nationalism at the ballot box alone. I think that's a mistake. Biblical deconstruction without reconstruction is not a strategy of protest. Rather, it's a strategy of cynicism. The Bible remains a point of rare common ground between Christian nationalists and Christians challenging Christian nationalism. This space is awkward and contentious, but it is nonetheless a shared space.

One of the things I've heard dozens of times from pastors and leaders over the past three years is that sermons are not enough for challenging biblical authoritarianism and misplaced loyalties to MAGA Jesus. This is especially true because of social media's ability to bombard congregants with misinformation for multiple hours a week. How can a fifteen-minute sermon keep up with the flood of spiritual hucksters and media fear mongers? The answer is that sermons can't keep up.

I don't want to despair or minimize the potential for sermons to change lives, but I do want to shoot it straight: we urgently need more spaces for sustained biblical study and theological education in congregations. Put another way, we need Vacation Bible School for adults. We need Sunday school classes. We need what one church I lectured at this year called "Winter Bible School." In these spaces we can unpack the six steps for challenging white Christian nationalism and practice studying the whole life of Jesus with a Christocentric hermeneutic of love and resistance.

Step five for challenging white Christian nationalism is to teach the whole life of Jesus—in public!

Questions for Reflection

1. Have you seen or experienced biblical authoritarianism?

2. In what ways do you think the Bible is important for challenging Christian nationalism?

3. Where do people in your community go to learn about the Bible?

4. How have you been taught to define the gospel?

5. What do you think it means to make public arguments about the Bible?

6. What would it look like to practice a Christocentric hermeneutic of love and resistance in your community?

Chapter 6

Building People Power to Challenge Christian Nationalism

One side has been readying for conflict for sixty years.

—Bradley Onishi[1]

IT IS ONE THING to break our silence about Christian nationalism and competently name what we are against. It is entirely another thing to mobilize a movement of people to build capacity and counter what we are against. Without the power of people any movement to counter Christian nationalism will be futile. The final step for challenging Christian nationalism is to build people power.

In his much-anticipated book, *Preparing for War: The Extremist History of White Christian Nationalism—and What Comes Next*, former Christian nationalist turned scholar of religion Bradley Onishi offers a sober forecast about America's future. I confess that, when I got my copy of Onishi's book, I frantically skipped to the final chapter to learn about "what comes next." Part of me

---

1. Onishi, *Preparing for War*, 215.

was relieved that Onishi doesn't offer bold predictions about the future. Another part of me was disturbed by Onishi's observation that adherents of Christian nationalism have been readying for conflict for sixty years (ever since it emerged as a reaction to the civil rights movement).

Onishi's warning is a reminder that Christian nationalism in the United States is something more than an ideology or theology. It is also a well-organized social movement of real people who wield enormous power over the church, our political system, and our life together. One example of this organizing power is Turning Point USA (TPUSA), a non-profit right-wing activist group led by the disgraced Jerry Falwell Jr.'s prodigy, Charlie Kirk.

Founded by the twenty-nine-year-old Kirk in 2012, TPU-SA has rapidly expanded its student movement into 3,500 high schools and college campuses to advance its three core beliefs: (1) the United States of America is the greatest country in the history of the world; (2) the US Constitution is the most exceptional political document ever written; and (3) capitalism is the most moral and proven economic system ever discovered.[2] Through a massive social media and podcast presence, TPUSA claims to have reached over one billion people to "play offense with a sense of urgency to win America's culture war."

In recent years, TPUSA has expanded its mission into "TPU-SA Faith" to infiltrate and recruit churches to advance the values of Christian nationalism. In fact, TPUSA now regularly holds "Pastor Summits" where hundreds gather to worship and hear dozens of far-right speakers offer strategies for taking America's government and schools back for God. Some of these summits have even waived registration fees and hotel costs for pastors and leaders in large cities like Phoenix and San Diego. TPUSA is a living illustration of how Christian nationalism is a well-funded and durable social movement. It is funded by a political and religious deep story that has been preparing for conflict for over six decades. It's hard not to despair when Christians challenging Christian nationalism seem to be getting out-organized and out-funded.

2. See https://www.tpusa.com/about.

To scale up and build people power against Christian nationalism we need a context out of which to organize and counter-recruit against organizations like TPUSA and their media empires. This work will not be easy. We also need what Jonathan Smucker calls a "leaderful" movement rather than a "leaderless" one.[3] This means building capacity and collective power through diverse change agents like pastors, congregants, scholars, lawyers, teachers, youth, non-profits, interfaith organizations, and parents, along with a diverse geographical collective of churches. While there are podcasters and faith-based organizations doing some of this organizing work already, here I wish to explore how congregations can become sites for mobilizing people power. Put bluntly, *we need to see congregations as a part of the solution rather than a part of the problem for challenging Christian nationalism.*

In this chapter, I will explore the role churches have to play and offer suggestions for building people power *in church.* The global church, I believe, is God's challenger movement against strange worship.

The Church and People Power: There's No Plan B

Christians challenging Christian nationalism are not without contexts and infrastructure for mobilizing people power against Christian nationalism's strange worship. One context that gets short shrift in this cultural moment is what the Apostle Paul called the *ekklesia,* or "assembly" of Christ followers. We now tiredly translate the Greek word *ekklesia* as "church." Frustratingly, as we know too well by now, some churches in the United State are ambassadors for strange worship; others are resisters of strange worship (but too often with a sense of paralysis about what to do about it).

I was recently sitting in a tense faculty meeting after a painful and tragic event in my community. While I was feeling the nearness of the church's brokenness, one of my senior colleagues took

3. Smucker, *Hegemony How-To,* 184–86.

the breath out of my lungs when he bluntly said: "God chose the church to work in. There's no plan B." This is a hard theological pill to swallow in this moment of church abuse, scandal, and de-churching. I won't waste any oxygen minimizing the harms some have experienced in the church. These harms are, in the fullest sense of the word, evil. Church abuse and power worship are an invitation to break silence and lament.

Again, it's okay to be angry at God and our Christian neighbors for strange worship *within* the church. Still, there's no plan B. There's no faith-based organization or government agency that can replace the church's mission of reconciliation. The fourth-century Roman emperor Constantine coercively built a Christian empire and it failed—miserably. Christian nationalism is an heir of this Constantinian legacy of power worship, and its imperial project will ultimately fail, too.

I believe that congregations across America are where God has pitched a tent to mobilize a challenger movement against strange worship (John 1:14). Yes, the church has many allies that participate in this work, but the church is the primary context for building people power, liturgies of resistance, and for participating in the ongoing life of God through the sacraments. It is not lost on me that this conviction has fallen out of favor among many of my friends and peers. Indeed, forty million people have stopped attending church over the past twenty-five years in the United States—tragically, all amid a pandemic of loneliness.[4] Some of the top reasons for dechurching are changing beliefs, instances of misogyny, and disagreement with the politics of the congregation.[5] While the "secular left" has become a viral boogie man to stoke fear in the media among Christian nationalists, recent data shows that evangelicals are, in fact, dechurching "at twice the frequency of those on the political left, almost catching up to the

---

4. Davis et al., *Great Dechurching*, 5. In the authors' words, "More people have left the church in the last twenty-five years than all the new people who became Christians from the First Great Awakening, Second Great Awakening, and Billy Graham crusades *combined*" (5).

5. See Fig. 11.1.

total percentage of those who have dechurched to the secular left."[6] Notably, the secular right is a space where Christian nationalism thrives, especially in rural areas of the United States.[7] We need to talk about this more.

To mobilize people power in congregations we also need to step back for a minute to ask: mobilize power toward what? A Nigerian peacebuilder I recently met reminded me how tricky this question is in the US context. She asked me, "How do we challenge Christian nationalism in the United States when its leaders and institutions are scattered across so many layers of the United States' institutions, and it doesn't have one singular leader?" She went on to observe, "In my context in Nigeria, we all know where the terror group Boko Haram lives and who is in charge. Christian nationalism in the United States is different since its power is diffused across many persons and institutions." This perceptive observation raises a question we need more clarity on. What institutions—*exactly*—are we trying to mobilize people power against?

One way to portray this diffused power dynamic is through an organizing tool called the pillars of power or pillars of support.[8] With this tool, we can think of Christian nationalism as an ideological, religious, and political system of power that sits atop supporting institutions like churches, religious leaders, media outlets, wealthy business leaders, politicians, education systems, and narratives of xenophobia and American exceptionalism embedded in our armed forces. These leaders and institutions supply authority and legitimacy to Christian nationalism. Certainly, there are other supporting pillars (like the judicial system), but the point is that if one of these pillars crumbles and withholds support then Christian nationalism's power and legitimacy will be neutralized or significantly undermined. We can map this out as follows:[9]

6. Davis et al., *Great Dechurching*, 31.

7. See Williams, "What Really Happens When Americans Stop Going to Church."

8. The idea was introduced by Robert L. Helvey but used by Gene Sharp and many others. See Sharp, *Sharp's Dictionary of Power and Struggle*, 220.

9. See "Pillars of Power."

Pillars of Power

Christian Nationalism

Institutions | Military/Police | Schools | Politicians | Businesses | Media | Churches

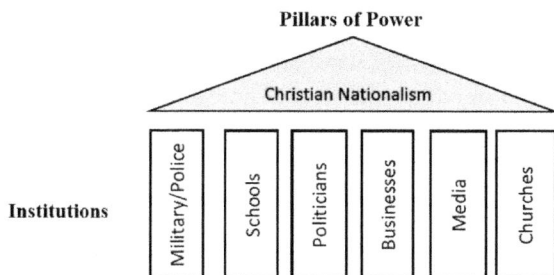

The pillars of power rely on a theory of power that was popularized in 1986 when a mass nonviolent popular protest erupted against President Ferdinand Marcos in the Philippines after he rigged an election. Onlookers called the mass popular movement "people power" and the term stuck. At the heart of people power is the conviction that power is not exclusively owned by politicians, theologians and pastors, the wealthy, and the military. Rather, power is fragile—the powerful are dependent on the peoples' compliance, cooperation, obedience, and consent. When consent is taken away, their power is toppled or disoriented.

The pillars of power are a hopeful reminder that we don't have to transform all of Christian nationalism's supporting institutions to minimize its threat to democracy, the church's witness, and human security. In an ideal world we'd build a coordinated peacebuilding movement that targets all six pillars, but that might be unrealistic. This book is about effective and realistic resistance. Toward this end, focusing on congregations and religious leaders to withdraw consent and passive obedience toward the values *and* policies of Christian nationalism is an important step forward. By focusing on churches, we may also initiate a trickle-up effect where public opinion shifts within other supporting pillars, including among educators, politicians, and those who control capital (which includes many Christians).

The bottom line is that Christian nationalism cannot flourish without churches and Christian influencers' consent. To challenge consent, we have to break silence and mobilize people power to shift Christian loyalties away from strange worship toward the whole life of Jesus. As Chenoweth and Stephan argue, when participation increases, success rates also increase. Congregations are strategically positioned for this work. There's no plan B.

In Many Languages: Pentecost and People Power

Recently, I visited a university to lecture on a pastoral approach to challenging Christian nationalism. During the morning session, we spent a few hours defining Christian nationalism and then spent the afternoon on action steps for a pastoral response. At the end of the morning session, we offered an open mic for questions. An elderly white man immediately took the microphone, and I could tell that he was agitated. Sure enough, he vulnerably shared, "I had no idea what I signed up for when I came here today in this room full of strangers. I have concerns about how patriotic my congregation has become, but I'm still a conservative Republican, and I feel like this seminar is just trying to make us a bunch of liberal Democrats." I gently responded that my goal was to invite Christians of all parties to become more like Jesus—not like Democrats. Still, the exchange shook me.

After lunch I was surprised to see that he stayed for my afternoon session. I could see that people at his table were having civil but energetic conversations with him, building trust. After my afternoon talk, we immediately found each other in the middle of the lecture hall. He said, "I hope you weren't offended by my comment. I had no idea what I was coming to today, but I learned a ton. I'm tired of singing patriotic songs in my church instead of worship songs. I think I've been wrong—I didn't realize what Christian nationalism is and how big it has become in my political party." Then he said this: "I don't know, I think maybe the Holy Spirit is just working on me today. I've got a lot to think about."

That moment left a mark on me. It reaffirmed for me that a church-led nonviolent resistance movement against Christian nationalism needs to be *leaderful* and *Spirit-full* (rather than strictly partisan). The story of Pentecost in Acts 2 offers us a dynamic paradigm for building just such a transformative leaderful and

Spirit-full movement. Too often we think of Pentecost as a reversal of the so-called curse of Babel in Genesis 11:1–9, where God mixed up the languages of a monolinguistic people who sought to build a culturally homogenous empire. We are taught to think of speaking in many languages as a curse because we're baptized into ethnocentric nationalism from a young age. We are taught to fear other languages and cultural groups as a threat to our way of life. Christian nationalism is an imperial project not unlike Babel; it is a political movement to build a fortified tower where whiteness and English dominate. God mixed up human languages at Babel to disrupt nationalism and empire-making. This is a blessing, not a curse.

Like Babel, Pentecost is God's rebuke of monocultural imperial projects like Christian nationalism. At Pentecost, God empowers the disciples to proclaim the gospel of God's in-breaking peace in the heart languages of Jews gathered in Jerusalem from around the Roman Empire. The entire scene builds off the disciples' earnest question in Acts 1:6: "Lord, is this the time when you will restore the kingdom to Israel?" At this point in the story, the disciples still seem to think that Jesus' power in the post-resurrection world will emerge as a violent rescue operation against Rome's occupation of Israel. Jesus redirects the disciples' expectations toward a new kind of power: the coming of the Holy Spirit for a mission of nonviolent "witness" to the ends of the earth (Acts 1:8).

Pentecost is the birthing of God's leaderful and Spirit-full challenger movement against power worship and "English-only" ideologies of exclusion and hate. Pentecost is an invitation for broad participation by diverse groups to celebrate cultural difference, rather than fear it. Pentecost is God's answer to cultural violence that leads to direct violence. It is an invitation for broad participation by diverse ethnicities to join God's challenger movement of overwhelming strange worship with people power soaked in God's love. Pentecost is an invitation to bear witness to the *whole life of Jesus* in many languages (Acts 2:17–35). It is the beginning of a revolution because the Holy Spirit is the engine that joins formerly alienated peoples in friendship with God and neighbor.

I have no doubt that God's enmity-crushing Holy Spirit was at work in that man's life after my lecture. I know this to be true because I could feel the Holy Spirit at work in me, too.

A Transformative Peacebuilding Approach to Challenging Christian Nationalism

To challenge Christian nationalism effectively we need a leaderful and a Spirit-full movement. We also need a peace-full movement (as in *full* of peace). We need a peace-full movement because peace is the way of Jesus, but also because we know from data that nonviolent resistance is more effective than direct violence at transforming conflict, toppling dictators, and leaving societies in a healthier state of democracy. In other words, a peace-full movement is a theological conviction *and* a strategic one.

As I argued in chapter 5, Christian nationalism is a form of violent extremism. Its theology of "us vs. them" can lead to terrorism, violent insurrection, "lost dog" attacks, and direct violence. Even in its softer versions, Christian nationalism legitimates structural and cultural violence, especially against women, queer, and Black and Brown bodies in the United States. The question before us is how to minimize harm, reduce violence, and rebuild structures that promote human flourishing.

I believe congregations can be platforms for transforming conflict and building peace, but to do that, in the words of Scot McKnight, we need to admit that "the Bible is not enough."[10] McKnight's provocative point is that the Bible's peace witness cannot be realized without improvisation and participation. To improvise, we need new conversation partners outside of the disciplines of theology and biblical studies. I think those conversation partners exist in the form of peacebuilding theorists and practitioners, or within the discipline of "peace studies."

As I've immersed myself in the literature of peace studies, I've found myself convicted that any serious church-led effort to

10. McKnight, *Bible Is Not Enough.*

challenge Christian nationalism must go through this literature. This conviction has only strengthened as I've watched countless rejecters of Christian nationalism offer their take on this moment seemingly without any awareness of this body of research (to be clear, the discipline of peace studies is new for me, too!). Part of the reason for this gap in our understanding is that peace studies scholars have invested significant energy on international peacebuilding, security studies, and the war on terror. Meanwhile, domestic extremism in the United States has grown under our feet. Still, their ideas are highly relevant for the US context as we improvise strategic change processes and develop a conceptual framework to challenge strange worship.

At the heart of transformative peacebuilding is the counter-cultural conviction that conflict is a good thing—an opportunity, a gift, and "potential catalyst for growth."[11] Peacebuilding, then, is not passive or idealistic, nor is it only for warring or for post-war contexts. Peacebuilding, according to Lisa Schirch, "seeks to prevent, reduce, transform, and help people recover from violence in all forms, even structural violence that has not yet led to massive civil unrest."[12] In this sense, peacebuilding is concerned with three realms of conflict: (1) pre-violence, or the months and years leading up to violence; (2) episodes of violence; and (3) post-violence, or the months and years following violence. The work of prevention *and* recovery are crucial for challenging Christian nationalism, but here I'm especially concerned with nurturing spaces that disrupt radicalization in the months and years leading up to violence. I will reflect on three points.

First, as far as I can tell, resisters and rejecters of Christian nationalism do not have shared understanding or clarity about *who* we are mobilizing to challenge Christian nationalism. Much of our shared work is being thrown to the winds of social media algorithms and the publishing industrial complex in search for ears to hear and eyes to see. That's good! But I think we can mobilize

---

11. Lederach, *Conflict Transformation*, 15.

12. Schirch, *Little Book of Strategic Peacebuilding*, 9.

people power in even more targeted ways by thinking more strategically about *who* we are mobilizing.

John Paul Lederach, who is a pioneer thinker in peacebuilding, calls this the "strategic who." The strategic who are influencers who can change public opinions and mobilize critical masses of people. Lederach likens the strategic "who" to yeast in a bread recipe. The amount of yeast is small, but makes the bread rise and transform. We need strategic leaders to mobilize resisters and rejecters and shift ambassadors' and accommodators' perspectives along the spectrum of allies toward peace and justice. To do that, we need to think thoughtfully about *where* in society we are drawing these leaders from in populations most affected by Christian nationalism. Lederach's emphasis on "critical yeast" is an important nuance for those who think we can challenge Christian nationalism through a "critical mass" of people alone.

Lederach diagrams these leaders in a pyramid with three levels: (1) top-level leaders like politicians, UN leaders, and high-visibility business and religious leaders; (2) mid-level leaders like academics, pastors, and lawyers; and (3) grassroots leaders like organizers, youth groups, teachers, non-profits, etc. A successful challenger movement, according to Lederach, builds horizontal capacity across relationships within each level, but also builds vertical capacity through coordinated relationships between top, middle, and grassroots levels.

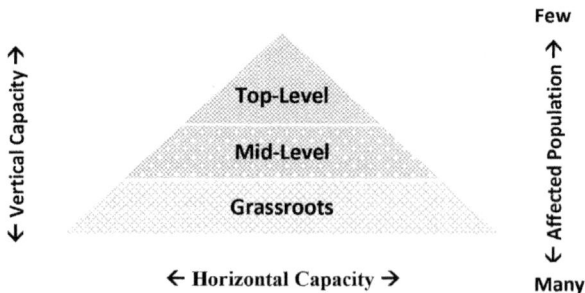

Lederach's pyramid invites us to be more precise about the strategic *who* and the strategic *where* for mobilizing leaders in our human collectives. Mid-level academics and pastors, religious liberty lawyers, and journalists are key to mobilizing some of this work but need to be careful to not create echo chambers detached from the grassroots along lines of class, privilege, and information silos. Moreover, Christians lobbying top-level leaders need to be careful to not convey that K-Street-style lobbying and ballot boxes are the only way to build peace and challenge strange worship. For those lobbying top-level leaders, my six postures that lead to strange worship in chapter 4 offer an important handrail.

In a country where many Christians are already leveraging their public voice, we need eyes, ears, and voices on the ground, and grassroots leaders are the most relationally attuned to what's happening below. The goal here is to identify and leverage infrastructure that "can sustain the peacebuilding process over the long term."[13] I believe that congregations and their supporting institutions provide this kind of durable infrastructure and platform. The challenge is to get them to "break silence" and to identify leaders in the middle and grassroots who can bring diverse actors across ecumenical lines to the table. That work before us is urgent.

Second, a transformative peacebuilding approach to challenging Christian nationalism can help us develop skills for not becoming incapacitated by episodes of strange worship in our midst. Instead, Lederach calls peacebuilders to a posture of curiosity—to see beyond the "presenting issues" or "episodes" of conflict toward the broader systems that gave birth to the conflict, or what he calls the "epicenter" of conflict. For example, if all we do is address the January 6 Capitol insurrection (the episode of conflict) without addressing the legacy of white supremacy (the epicenter of conflict), then our vision for challenging Christian nationalism will be shortsighted. Here, Lederach invites us to "be short-term responsive and long-term strategic," meaning that we need to address the episode of the January 6 insurrection *and* its epicenter rooted in white supremacy.[14]

According to PRRI, 85 percent of white adherents of Christian nationalism believe that "discrimination against white Americans

13. Lederach, *Building Peace,* 60.
14. Lederach, *Little Book of Conflict Transformation,* 50.

has become as big a problem as discrimination against Black Americans and other minorities."[15] Other studies have shown that Christian nationalism's support for political violence is shaped by white identity, perceived victimhood, and support for the QAnon movement.[16] The January 6 insurrection is merely a symptom or episode of a much deeper epicenter of conflict rooted in white supremacy and the myth of racial progress in the United States.

The risk is that we miss the forest for trees, that January 6 becomes a distraction from longer-term work that disrupts white supremacy, including racial progress narratives that fuel white grievances.[17] This demands patience for long-term peacebuilding, along with reclaiming congregations as a transformative platform for violence prevention and recovery at the level of episodes and epicenters of conflict.

Finally, a transformative peacebuilding approach to challenging Christian nationalism can help us foreground relationships for building horizontal and vertical capacity. The work of relationship building is even more pressing as traditional human collectives are gutted by the neoliberal order. Building relationships amid a pandemic of loneliness is not a soft or idealistic form of peacebuilding. Rather, it is a targeted strategy for countering radicalization and for building horizontal capacity in diverse coalitions of people for violence prevention and recovery. As Schirch argues, "Relationships are a form of power or *social capital*. When people connect and form relationships, they are more likely to cooperate together to constructively address conflict."[18]

Congregations, along with their supporting institutions and allies, are already strategically positioned to create spaces for building relationships at the grassroots. Pastors and leaders should openly speak into Christian nationalism in these spaces by publicly naming diverse coalitions of churches as a "strategic who" for challenging it. In doing so, they will inject new purpose and meaning

15. See "Christian Nation?"

16. See Armaly et al., "Christian Nationalism and Political Violence."

17. Dehrone et al., *Renewing American Democracy,* 12.

18. Schirch, *Strategic Peacebuilding,* 9.

into our Sunday gatherings: yes, we gather to worship God, but we also gather to build relationships to challenge third order suffering and improvise God's in-breaking peace in our neighborhoods. This work is not always easy, but it is the kind of relational approach we need to challenge Christian nationalism—mobilizing people power cannot be done on social media alone.

To challenge Christian nationalism we need a leaderful, spirit-full, peace-full, *and relationship-full movement.*

Public Faith: Building Vertical Capacity to Challenge Strange Worship

I often tell people that living in the city of Chicago was the best theology class I've ever taken. My wife and I moved to Chicago in 2006 and worshiped for seven years in a multicultural Christian community on the corner of Pratt and Ashland in Rogers Park. When I left the congregation, we were passing the peace of Christ in seven languages. This community and the city of Chicago changed my life.

When I moved to Rogers Park, I was still reeling from the atrocities of the Iraq war. I was rightly cynical about political power and militarism. As I leaned into my new-found Anabaptist Christian identity, I quickly embraced a spirit of non-participation in our political system as a strategy of protest. What I quickly learned as I helped to resettle refugee families, worked with African American youth, and witnessed gun violence, is that I'm not the one getting jacked by the system. My white and male body gave me a pass, a kind of immunity from the structural violence that plagued my neighborhood. Once you see structural violence, you can't unsee it. This is the real meaning of being "woke."

I know I'm not the only privileged Christian in the past twenty years to experience an "awakening" to injustice. The Black Lives Matter movement, #MeToo, and the election of Donald Trump have awoken a critical mass of people in privileged communities who are now concerned about injustice. That's a good thing. Still, there's a body of Christians out there who are holding onto an apolitical posture expressed in clichés like "Jesus wasn't a Republican or a Democrat." This is an easy thing to say if you're a person of privilege in the United States. After all, most of us privileged white folks don't go to bed at night afraid of ICE raids, police brutality, deportations, evictions, hate speech, environmental degradation, lack of clean drinking water, or our subordinate space in America's racial caste system. This is where the language of Jesus' "third way" among some white Christians has become sanitized. The descriptor *third way* was not meant as an invitation to become neutral toward the powers that be. Rather, it is an invitation to speak and act prophetically to create movements that dismantle them. In the words of the Poor People's Campaign, "It's not about left and right; it's about right and wrong." Sometimes that means taking sides.

During the 2010s more people took to the streets around the globe to protest injustice than at any other point in human history. From Tunisia to Wall Street, from Tahrir Square to São Paulo, from Hong Kong to Turkey, and from Washington, DC to Minneapolis—the list of popular uprisings goes on. Yet very few of these movements cultivated the long-term change they hoped for; in fact, many resulted in the opposite of what they hoped for.

From internal critics of these popular uprisings, we've learned that there is one way we can be different. We can be different by not being afraid to build some vertical capacity and leaderful representation. Too often progressive leaders are critical of hierarchy, power, and leadership. Yet without some vertical capacity, movements often fail. As the Egyptian human rights activist Hossam Bahgat puts it, "Organise. Create an organised movement. And don't be afraid of representation . . . We thought representation was elitism, but actually it is the essence of democracy."[19] Building vertical capacity remains a controversial idea among many resisters and rejecters of Christian nationalism. I've even heard from some prominent theologians that the so-called Christian left is merely mirroring the power worship of the right. While I mostly disagree with this analysis, congregations urgently need guidance

19. See Bevins, "Mass Protest Decade."

for how to build capacity and leverage democracy in responsible and life-giving ways.

To build vertical capacity without becoming coopted by state power we need to have a clear vision of the biblical vision for human flourishing, or what the Catholic tradition calls the "common good." The biblical vision for human flourishing gives us a mirror to hold up to epicenters and episodes of conflict. It also gives us a vision for being "long-term strategic." Successful challenger movements need a different understanding of time—centered on an idealized, justice- and hope-filled future. From this utopian vision of the future, it is believed that successful challenger movements find ways to incarnate visions of a better world in the present. Without such visions, social movements will ultimately fail.

I think the Hebrew word *shalom* best captures God's vision for human flourishing. *Shalom* is the Hebrew word for peace in the Old Testament, but it has little to do with inner personal peace. Shalom is about cosmic and corporate wholeness, well-being, intactness of community, relief from stress, and liberation from oppressors.[20] Shalom is closely associated with justice in the Bible and has two sides: aid for the needy and breaking the power of the oppressor. The Genesis creation account gives us our first glimpse into the cosmic wholeness of shalom when Adam and Eve live in peace with God, each other, and the created order. This is the world God desires—a world where humans live in peace with God, each other, and creation.

The Bible tells the story of how, from the moment humans turned to their own way, God works to restore shalom to creation to overwhelm the power of sin. God's story of restoring shalom to creation happens through the nation of Israel and climactically through Israel's messiah-king, Jesus Christ. When Jesus proclaimed the kingdom of God, he was signaling that God's liberating shalom is drawing near. When Jesus taught his disciples to pray, "Your kingdom come, your will be done, on earth as it is in heaven" (Matt 6:10), he was teaching them to pray boldly for God's peace and justice to fully arrive in this world. The New

---

20. On the meaning of shalom, see Yoder, *Shalom*.

Testament even ends with a justice- and hope-filled vision of God's shalom. In Revelation 21, John talks about Jesus' return at the end of history when God will "make all things new" and restore God's home among humans to "wipe every tear from their eyes. Death will be no more; mourning and crying and pain will be no more" (Rev 21:1–5). I want to live in that world—*now*. From shalom at creation to shalom in the new creation, this is the narrative arc of the Bible.

Public faith requires us to be long-term strategic about improvising God's shalom now. It requires us to have a different understanding of time. In 2018 I had the privilege of attending a Poor People's Campaign event at the US Capitol building in Washington, DC with my then ten-month-old son to protest the war economy. As clergy lined up to march into senators' offices with a message of shalom, my brother Art Laffin from the Dorothy Day Catholic Workers House saw my son and me out of the corner of his eye. While singing hymns of faithful resistance, Art slowly and very seriously left the assembly and walked straight toward us. Without acknowledging me, Art walked straight up to my son Bo, got down in his face, and said, "Bo, I'm doing this for you. I'm doing this today to help make a better world for your generation." As I watched Art sing his way back to the clergy and ultimately to jail that night, I thought to myself: *This is a man who understands what it means to be long-term strategic.* Art knew that his direct actions that day might not bring down the system in one swipe. But Art knew that by dramatically improvising God's in-breaking kingdom of peace that he was chipping away at the system, which will ultimately give way to God's shalom-filled world.

The theologian Miroslav Volf talks about two kinds of public faith. One is idleness and the other is coercion.[21] Christians of all stripes exist on a spectrum between the poles of idle neutrality and religion by coercion. Both approaches to public faith are flawed because the former fails to love our vulnerable neighbors as ourselves and the latter lords power over others. For Volf, faith by coercion is a "thinned out faith" because it weaponizes the church's public

21. Volf, *Public Faith*, 23–54.

witness. Faith by coercion leverages power through violence rather than nonviolent persuasion and bearing witness to the life of Jesus. (Think of the January 6 insurrection and conspiracy theories of a stolen election.)

Christianity by coercion is not going to go away anytime soon. In his recent book *Defending Democracy from Its Christian Enemies*, David Gushee argues that Christians around the world favor "authoritarian and reactionary political trends that pose a grave threat to open and free democracy . . . Christians turn out to be among the leading threats to democracy in much of the world."[22] As we navigate these dynamics, it is tempting to name the church as the problem rather than the solution to these authoritarian tendencies. I feel this dynamic, too. But here I'm in strong agreement with Volf that the "cure against Christian violence is not less of the Christian faith, but, in a carefully qualified sense, *more* of the Christian faith."[23] The problem is not the inherent violence of religion or Christianity per se but "the *quality* of religious commitment."[24] This is again a space where congregations can step up to provide a leaderful approach to spiritual formation that challenges dominion theology's strange worship.

Determining the characteristics of the public faith that Christians challenging Christian nationalism are called to embrace is humbling: we live in a time that is very different than the earliest Christians in many ways. For one, empires in our modern context are armed with weapons of mass destruction, and we Christians living under these empires today *do* have political power—the power to vote, to organize, and the freedom to flex our dissident voice without fear of incarceration. We can sit idly with that power, or we can leverage it for the common good. I want to propose that Christians challenging Christian nationalism have a moral duty to participate in the democratic process to reduce violence and minimize harm to our neighbors. We should mobilize our collective power with a posture of suspicion and ambivalence toward state

---

22. Gushee, *Defending Democracy*, 1.

23. Volf, *Public Faith*, 40.

24. Volf, *Public Faith*, 20.

power rather than trust and absolute loyalty. Our ultimate collective loyalty is to the life and teachings of Jesus. This is a public faith of witness and persuasion with the weapons of love, not coercion.

When I moved to the Saint Joseph River watershed five years ago to teach at Anabaptist Mennonite Biblical Seminary (AMBS) in Elkhart, Indiana, I had a lot of stigmas about small towns in the rustbelt. I assumed that small towns in the rustbelt are predominantly white and Trump country. I couldn't have been more wrong. During my first semester at AMBS in 2018, news broke of a Latino man who was brutally beaten by police on camera in the Elkhart Police Station. The beating was especially newsworthy because the mayor's son watched the beating while on duty. The beating prompted *Pro Publica* and the *South Bend Tribune* to investigate reports of police brutality by the African American and Latino community going back to the 1980s. They found that residents in Elkhart are more likely to be shot by a police officer than residents in New York City and discovered years of officer promotions after they were accused of brutality. The news was even featured on National Public Radio.[25]

After this news broke some of my colleagues decided to do something. Mind you, some of these colleagues are radical Anabaptists, meaning they are extremely suspicious of partisan politics and, at times, political participation. For the next year, they mobilized a diverse coalition of leaders to elect Elkhart's first African American mayor. Their candidate of choice, Rod Roberson, is a Christian businessman who knows everyone and their dog. Rod ran on three things: (1) equitable investment across the city; (2) police reform; and (3) restoring the city's community center for youth. In November of 2019 Rod won with the help of a leaderful movement, including women in churches who functioned as key communicators in the community. Rod's leadership has done much to restore public trust in the police department. He is now working with community leaders to rebuild a once vibrant historic Black neighborhood that was razed to the ground by the federal Urban Renewal program with the promise of redevelopment.

25. See Inskeep, "Indiana Police."

That promise never happened—until now, under the leadership of Mayor Roberson.[26]

The election of Rod is, for me, an ongoing case study of public faith that builds vertical capacity. I recently asked one of my colleagues who helped elect Rod how it feels to have some power. He smirked and said this: "In the words of Howard Zinn, 'It's impossible to be neutral on a moving train.' What kind of passenger are you? We all have power. It's okay to engage in the public sphere without entirely identifying with it. We can be critical care takers of our faith tradition and with public life." I think there's wisdom in this: taking a side to reduce harm in society through democracy is not the same thing as pledging loyalty to the state or a political party. We can be ambivalent toward partisan loyalties *and* leverage state power toward human flourishing.

Every generation must grapple with public faith for new contexts and challenges. In our cultural moment, silence, or idle neutrality, before democracy's dominionist Christian enemies is a form of compliance, and it's not the privileged who will suffer.

Resistance Begets Resistance

The thing about breaking silence about Christian nationalism is that you never know how the Holy Spirit will move. This past spring, I was teaching a four-week short course called "Resisting Christian Nationalism with the Gospel of Peace." My students were diverse, including pastors, lay persons, doctors, lawyers, businesspersons, farmers, retired couples, and one former Obama administration official. These students showed up with their game faces on. One of my students, Jane, even wrote an op-ed for her local paper in Iowa City about Christian nationalism. She titled it, "So, just what would a Christian nation look like?"[27] The article was picked up by Yahoo News and, the last time I checked, it had 1,786 comments. Resistance begets resistance.

---

26. See Marzurek, "Elkhart Officials."

27. Yoder-Short, "So, Just What Would a Christian Nation Look Like?

Step six for challenging Christian nationalism is to mobilize "people power." Ideally, I think this mobilization should be done in coordination with diverse local congregations with the support of their national and global institutions and their allies. This means creating shared spaces (ideally ecumenical ones) to break silence, define white Christian nationalism, discuss the boundaries of political idolatry, and confront and challenge the structural realities that brought us to this place of polarization (especially disinformation on social media and third order suffering). A church-led response to challenging Christian nationalism must publicly name these dynamics in a posture of empathy *and* prophetic critique that is rooted in bearing witness to the *whole* life of Jesus.

Yes, some churches are a part of the problem. At the same time, it's also true that some churches are or can become a major part of the solution. We need a leaderful, spirit-full, peace-full, and relationship-full movement with both horizontal and vertical capacity to challenge Christian nationalism.

Questions for Reflection

1. Do you have any "aha" moments from this chapter?
2. What do you think the role of the Holy Spirit is in building a challenger movement?
3. What do you think it means to build a "leaderful" movement?
4. Who are pillars of power that support Christian nationalism in your community?
5. Have you experienced building vertical capacity in a faith community before? What went well? What didn't go well?

Chapter 7

An Invitation to Get in the Way

"Feeling good, not engaging in violence, or being willing to die,
when you have not achieved the goals of your struggle, does not
change the fact that you have failed."

—Gene Sharp[1]

I'm a child of the 1990s in Eastern Washington State. Living
in Seattle's rain shadow meant listening to lots of Seattle-based
grunge bands like Nirvana, Pearl Jam and Alice and Chains. It also
meant growing up on the red side of the state, where right-wing
activity was a relatively normal part of life. I remember neo-Nazis'
annual march on downtown Coeur d'Alene. I remember watching the FBI's siege of Ruby Ridge on television from my family's
cabin on the other side of the Selkirk Mountains in North Idaho.
I also remember hearing about neighborhoods on the news that
got anonymously pamphleteered with neo-Nazi recruitment propaganda or antisemitic materials. At the time, these right-wing
events felt fringe and distant. Not so anymore.

---

1. Sharp, *Waging Nonviolent Struggle*, 436.

We are living amid a protracted conflict in the United States—what author Jeff Sharlet calls "a slow civil war."[2] This conflict is not new. The epicenter of this conflict is white supremacy, and its deep story goes beyond Trumpism and 1776. Trumpism is merely a symptom of this deep story and has served as a powerful vector for mainstreaming white supremacist hate and xenophobia in the aftermath of significant cultural and demographic shifts in the US after the election of America's first African American president, the Black Lives Matter movement, and the legalization of same-sex marriage through *Obergefell v. Hodges*.

The danger for anyone challenging Christian nationalism is giving into despair and paralysis. Sometimes it feels like we are all sitting together in our grade school classroom when the fire alarm goes off. I remember covering my ears at times because of the piercing sound. Instead of getting up and following our teacher outside, we are all stuck in our chairs listening to the alarm bells in a state of panic.

To get up from our chairs, we need help. That's what this book is about. The stakes are high. Democracy is under immediate threat by its Christian enemies and the church's public witness is already tarnished. As I type this conclusion, PRRI dropped new data about threats to American democracy. They found that 38 percent of Americans believe that things have gotten so far off track in the US that "we need a leader who is willing to break some rules if that's what it takes to set things right."[3] The work ahead to challenge Christian authoritarianism is one of reconstruction and innovation and will demand resilience. Failure by way of silence is not an option. On our own we don't have much power, but together we are powerful. As my friend Andre Stoner from Faith in Indiana asks: "Will we be spectators and pundits? Or will we take the risk of becoming agents and architects?"

This book is an invitation to get in the way—to take the risk of becoming agents and architects of a better church and a better world.

2. Sharlet, *Undertow*.

3. See "Threats to American Democracy."

134

The Six Steps and Global Christianity

Over the past three years I've had the privilege of working through the six steps for challenging Christian nationalism with hundreds of pastors and leaders from urban and rural contexts in the United States, Canada, Ethiopia, South Korea, Ghana, Colombia, Nigeria, Kenya, Pakistan, Indonesia, Malaysia, England, Australia, and New Zealand. I can't promise that these steps are perfect or watertight, but I can promise that they are relevant for the United States and other global contexts. In fact, I was completely taken off guard when my colleagues in Ethiopia and South Korea asked me to lecture on Christian nationalism. For these contexts, I stayed focused on what's happening in the US and to my surprise my audiences found deep resonance and multiple analogues for their own contexts.

From my students, I've also learned firsthand how rare it is for Christians to gather and discuss how ethnocentric nationalism is harming the church's public witness around the globe. Christian nationalism is the church's elephant in the room. To talk about our elephant, we need spaces to break silence, educate, and organize. While this book is mostly focused on the unique nuances of white Christian nationalism in the US context, I'm confident that the six steps can be contextualized for Christians dealing with power worship in many other contexts. We are better together, and we have much to learn from one another.

Grassroots Anti-Idol Practices
that Challenge Strange Worship

In chapter 4 I talked about how idolatry is a process, not a moment. Similarly, radicalization is a process of "getting caught up in the moment." On average, according to data on domestic terrorism in the United States, it takes five years for someone to radicalize. This means we have about five years to "get in the way." Part of the church's mission in this moment is to get in the way. One way to get in the way of strange worship and radicalization is to think about anti-idol practices that challenge strange worship.

Getting in the way is important because, as Stephen Fowl argues, idolatry is "a habit that, once it begins, is ever more difficult to recognize, let alone break."[4] One part of the work ahead of us is to make idols recognizable before they take hold of our lives; the other part is to break them. Here I offer twelve practices that interrupt habits that lead to strange worship. This list is not exhaustive. Rather, it's intended as a starting place. When done in community, these habits and practices are an inoculant against and interrupter of strange worship.

1. We resist strange worship when we to take exceptional care of our spiritual selves and mental health.

2. We resist strange worship when we practice mindfulness about our loyalty to partisan allegiances and the kingdoms of this world.

3. We resist strange worship when we offer generous hospitality to friends and strangers.

4. We resist strange worship when we practice generosity with our wealth and possessions.

5. We resist strange worship when we intentionally build diverse relationship networks to build horizontal capacity.

6. We resist strange worship when we partake in or facilitate cross-cultural experiences.

7. We resist strange worship when we pray for our enemies.

8. We resist strange worship when we periodically fast from social media and educate others about misinformation, brain hacking, and fake news.

9. We resist strange worship when we disrupt racial progress narratives.

---

4. Fowl, *Idolatry*, 27.

10. We resist strange worship when we gain skills for dialogue and empathic resistance.

11. We resist strange worship when we challenge biblical authoritarianism and create space for sustained and serious study of the whole life of Jesus.

12. We resist strange worship when we use our public voice to build vertical capacity to reduce violence and minimize harm toward our vulnerable neighbors.

Together, these steps can help to inoculate ourselves and communities from strange worship. While developing these twelves steps, I was tempted to offer rationale and commentary for each step. Instead, I've intentionally chosen to leave them open-ended for discussion. I've hat-tipped each of these ideas in this book at some point and trust they will speak for themselves. Here, I only wish to make one point: mindfulness is the opposite of absent-mindedness. One way to be mindful about our relationship with the kingdoms of this world is to look to our spiritual ancestors for wisdom and formation.

One ancient Jewish way to practice mindfulness about power worship was to pray the Shema every day (Deut 6:4–9). The Shema offered Jews the key to spiritual formation and flourishing. It is no accident that Jesus also prayed the Shema (Matt 22:34–40; Mark 12:28–31; Luke 10:25–28). When asked what is the first and greatest commandment, Jesus nuanced the Shema with Leviticus 19:18 to also place emphasis on neighborly love:

> Hear, O Israel, the Lord our God, the Lord is one.
> Love the Lord your God with all your heart, with all your soul, with all your mind, and with all your strength. (Deut 6:4–5)
>
> The second is this: Love your neighbor as yourself. (Lev 19:18)
>
> There is no commandment greater than these.

For Jesus, loving God and neighbor is the center of discipleship. One way for us to resist strange worship is to pray like Jesus prayed;

to pray the Shema multiple times a day to resist competing loyalties that distract us from loving God and neighbor.

Three Final Questions

Before putting some closure on this book, three questions about challenging Christian nationalism deserve reflection.

First, What if I'm An Introvert, Can I Really Make a Difference?

This question is an important one, especially for the introverts out there like me. We are living in a moment where the ideal activist marches at rallies, writes a book, has thousands of Twitter followers, and is a dynamic speaker. These ideals are not realistic for most of us and *that's okay!* To be a resister or rejecter of Christian nationalism you don't have to fit the mold of the ideal activist. I don't know of anyone who has thought about this dynamic more than Dorcas Cheng-Tozun.

In her book *Social Justice for the Sensitive Soul: How to Change the World in Quiet Ways,* Cheng-Tozun talks about the "Activist Ideal" that "asks us to always prioritize the needs of those we are serving above our own."[5] Cheng-Tozun argues that this ideal is actually impossible and unhealthy—indeed, "No one is the ideal activist." Instead of trying to live up to this illusory ideal, Cheng-Tozun invites sensitive souls to "be activists exactly as we are" since we "become agents of change not simply by what we do but also by who we are."[6] In the words of Kurt Cobain, "Come as you're." I commend Cheng-Tozun's book for the introverts out there looking for practical ways to participate in change making, including in quiet ways.

5. Cheng-Tozun, *Social Justice for the Sensitive Soul,* 34.
6. Cheng-Tozun, *Social Justice for the Sensitive Soul,* 38–39.

Second, Can Violent Extremists Change Their Minds?

The United States is experiencing a surge in domestic extremism. Right-wing extremists, for example, have organized 267 plots resulting in 91 fatalities since 2015.[7] During this same period, far-left violence accounted for sixty-six violent acts leading to nineteen deaths. Strikingly, right now about a quarter of all Americans (23 percent) agree that "because things have gotten so far off track, true American patriots may have to resort to violence in order to save our country."[8] This number is up from 15 percent in only two years since 2021. The threat of violent extremism has even led the Department of Homeland Security to expand research into domestic extremism.[9]

Research on how to deradicalize and disengage individuals from extremist groups is in embryonic form. However, we know from data that deradicalization and disengagement is possible. For example, researchers with START's Profiles in Individual Radicalization in the United States analyzed 2,226 people who engaged in extremist crimes and found that about 300 of these perpetrators disengaged from violent extremism in some way. In about a third of these cases, individuals stopped committing crimes but remained ideologically radicalized.

While deradicalization does not work for everyone, researchers are identifying interventions that reduce violence and engagement. One study found that "inoculative messaging" (or counternarratives) that warn against extremist groups can prevent engagement and radicalization before it happens.[10] Another study showed the significance of former extremist group members (or "formers"), who are now shepherding extremist group members toward disengagement and new identities.[11] This makes me won-

---

7. O'Harrow et al., "Rise of Domestic Extremism."

8. See "Threats to American Democracy."

9. Ainsley, "Biden DHS Plans."

10. See Braddock, "Vaccinating Against Hate."

11. See DeMichele et al., "Research and Evaluation on Domestic Radicalization."

der: a lot of us are "former" Christian nationalists or members of churches that embraced power worship in soft and hard versions. I like how my friend David Cramer thinks about this. He argues that we should add a fifth category of "repenters" to Whitehead and Perry's spectrum of ambassadors, accommodators, resisters, and rejecters of Christian nationalism.[12] What would it look like for some of us who are "formers" and "repenters" to serve as consultants and possibly even prayerfully shepherd Christian nationalists into new Christian identities centered on the whole life of Jesus? I'm guessing that many readers of this book are formers and don't even realize it!

Organizations like Life after Hate are assembling significant resources for the work of violence intervention and disengagement.[13] In addition, the church is literally built on the "inoculative messaging" of the gospel of peace. The gospel of peace is our intervention and Paul is our paradigm of life after hate, a violent extremist whose encounter with the risen Jesus set him on a path of reconciling humans to God *and* humans to one another. Reclaiming and centering the whole gospel in our congregations *is the work of inoculative messaging and violence intervention.*

Third, Can Extremism Be a Good Thing?

This question is a tricky one in this cultural moment of polarization and mudslinging. There's a cultural perception among many Americans that extremism is an inherently bad thing. Some even aim to avoid political extremes by appealing to a mushy centrist space in the middle that purportedly defies the trappings of the Republican vs. Democrat spectrum. Others, especially on the right, incessantly demonize progressives as "the radical left."

Scholars who study social movements, however, observe that the radicalization of one's political or theological convictions "can be an important precursor to meaningful social change." The

12. Cramer, "I Was a Christian Nationalist," 10.
13. See https://www.lifeafterhate.org/resources/.

problem is when people "feel that using violence in service of those views is not only justified but also recognized and celebrated."[14] Extremism, then, can harness energy and anger at injustice for the common good. It only becomes a problem when it is used to promote fear, hate, and violence. As the Rev. Dr. Martin Luther King Jr. asked in his *Letter from a Birmingham Jail,* "the question is not whether we will be extremists, but what kind of extremists we will be. Will we be extremists for hate or for love? Will we be extremists for the preservation of injustice or for the extension of justice?"[15]

Christians, as Dr. King goes on to argue, follow Jesus Christ who "was an extremist for love, truth and goodness . . . the nation and the world are in dire need of creative extremists." [16] The answer for challenging Christian nationalism's strange worship is more nonviolent creative extremists, not less.

A Personal Invitation to Get in the Way

In case you are still left wondering what *you* can do after finishing this book to participate in the work of challenging Christian nationalism, here are six suggestions:

1. Schedule a one-on-one with a friend, family member, or neighbor to discuss your takeaways from this book. I encourage you to start with resisters or rejecters in your community.

2. Write a prayer of lament that captures your anger and frustration about this moment and commit to praying it every day for a year.

3. Take a personal retreat for a few hours at your favorite coffee shop or park to do a personal inventory for how you can implement the twelve anti-idol practices in your life and community to resist strange worship.

14. Quoted in Abrams, "Deradicalizing Domestic Extremists."
15. April 16, 1963. I take the quote from Washington, ed., *I Have a Dream,* 94.
16. Washington, ed., *I Have a Dream,* 94.

4. Organize a small group in your congregation or social network to work through the six steps for challenging Christian nationalism.

5. Meet with your pastor or another leader in your community to encourage them to break silence.

6. Discern who runs things in your county and city. Who are pillars of power that decide what kind of county you live in? Explore ways you can help to build horizontal and vertical capacity to build peace, reduce violence, and promote policies for the common good.

A Call and Commissioning for the Resistance

I wish to close this book with a call and commissioning for the resistance. I invite you to respond to these questions on your own and/or in communities of fellowship.

Question: In a world of strange worship, will you break silence in your community to challenge white Christian nationalism?

Response: With God's help, I/we will.

Question: In a world of strange worship, will you harness your anger at injustice in a posture of lament and pray for God to change things?

Response: With God's help, I/we will.

Question: In the face of Christian nationalism's threat to democracy and the church's integrity, will you help others in your network define and understand Christian nationalism as you are able?

Response: With God's help, I/we will.

Question: In a world gutted by the neoliberal order, will you stand with those in your community experiencing third order suffering?

Response: With God's help, I/we will.

Question: In a polarized world, will you do your best—only when it is safe—to offer empathic resistance toward power worshipers?

Response: With God's help, I/we will.

Question: In a world of competing loyalties, do you promise to pledge allegiance to the God who raised Jesus from the dead and gave him the name that is above every name?

Response: With God's help, I/we will.

Question: In a world of violent extremism, will you bear witness to the whole life of Jesus in public and quiet ways as a counter narrative to violent extremism?

Response: With God's help, I/we will.

Question: In a world of activist ideals, will you commit to prioritizing your mental health and spiritual formation so that as you grow in God's word and wisdom, you may become an agent of mercy and justice?

Response: With God's help, I/we will.

Question: In a world of biblical authoritarianism, will you help protect the vulnerable in your community who are most at risk of experiencing harm from Christian nationalism?

Response: With God's help I/we will.

Question: In a world of fear and hate, do you promise to pray for your enemies, recognizing that the God we serve desires those who desire idols?

Response: With God's help, I/we will.

Question: Finally, as a citizen of God's kingdom living in the kingdoms of this world, will you collaborate with other Christians and allies to create spaces for dialogue, sharing wisdom, and peacebuilding?

Response: With God's help I/we will.

Amen.

Bibliography

Abrams, Zara. "Deradicalizing Domestic Extremists." *American Psychological Association* 52 (2021). https://www.apa.org/monitor/2021/07/cover-domestic-extremists.

Ainsley, Julia. "Biden DHS Plans to Expand Grants for Studying, Preventing Domestic Violent Extremism." *NBC News,* February 12, 2021. https://www.nbcnews.com/politics/national-security/biden-dhs-plans-expand-grants-studying-preventing-domestic-violent-extremism-n1257550.

Arendt, Hannah. *The Origins of Totalitarianism.* New York: Harvest, 1968.

Armaly, Miles T., et al. "Christian Nationalism and Political Violence: Victimhood, Racial Identity, Conspiracy, and Support for the Capitol Attacks." *National Library of Medicine* 44 (2022) 937–60. https://www.ncbi.nlm.nih.gov/pmc/articles/PMC8724742/.

Baker, Joseph O., et al. "Crusading for Moral Authority: Christian Nationalism and Opposition to Science." *Sociological Forum* 35 (2020) 587–607.

Barclay, John M. G. *Paul and the Power of Grace.* Grand Rapids: Eerdmans, 2020.

———. "Snarling Sweetly: Josephus on Images and Idolatry." In *Idolatry: False Worship in the Bible, Early Judaism and Christianity,* edited by Stephen C. Barton, 73–87. New York: T. & T. Clark, 2007.

Bevins, Vincent. "The Mass Protest Decade: Why Did the Street Movements of the 2010s Fail?" *The Guardian.* October 10, 2023. https://www.theguardian.com/world/2023/oct/10/the-mass-protest-decade-why-did-the-street-movements-of-the-2010s-fail.

Bleiweis, Robin, et al. "Women of Color and the Wage Gap." Center for American Progress, November 17, 2021. https://www.americanprogress.org/article/women-of-color-and-the-wage-gap/.

Braddock, Kurt. "Vaccinating Against Hate: Using Attitudinal Inoculation to Confer Resistance to Persuasion by Extremist Propaganda." *Terrorism and Political Violence* 34 (2022) 240–62. https://www.tandfonline.com/doi/abs/10.1080/09546553.2019.1693370.

Braucher, David. "Fake News: Why We Fall For It." *Psychology Today*, December 28, 2016. https://www.psychologytoday.com/us/blog/contemporary-psychoanalysis-in-action/201612/fake-news-why-we-fall-it.

Brueggemann, Walter. "The Costly Loss of Lament." In *The Psalms and the Life of Faith*, edited by Patrick D. Miller, 98–111. Minneapolis: Fortress, 1995.

———. *Prayers for a Privileged People*. Nashville: Abingdon, 2008.

Cabral, Sam, and Tara McKelvey. "Guy Reffit: Capitol Rioter Turned in by Son Gets 87 Months in Prison." *BBC*, August 1, 2022. https://www.bbc.com/news/world-us-canada-62382492.

Câmara, Hélder. *Spiral of Violence*. London: Sheed and Ward, 1971.

Charles, Mark. *Unsettling Truths: The Ongoing, Dehumanizing Legacy of the Doctrine of Discovery*. Downers Grove, IL: InterVarsity, 2019.

Cheng-Tozun, Dorcas. *Social Justice for the Sensitive Soul: How to Change the World in Quiet Ways*. Minneapolis: Broadleaf, 2023.

Chenoweth, Erica, and Maria J. Stephan. *Why Civil Resistance Works: The Strategic Logic of Nonviolent Conflict*. New York: Columbia University Press, 2011.

Choi, Matthew. "Trump: Military Will Defend Border from Caravan 'Invasion.'" *Politico*, October 29, 2018. https://www.politico.com/story/2018/10/29/trump-military-caravan-migrants-945683.

"A Christian Nation? Understanding the Threat of Christian Nationalism to American Democracy and Culture." Public Religion Research Institute, February 8, 2023. https://www.prri.org/research/a-christian-nation-understanding-the-threat-of-christian-nationalism-to-american-democracy-and-culture/.

Clapp, Rodney. *Naming Neoliberalism: Exposing the Spirit of Our Age*. Minneapolis: Fortress, 2021.

Cooper-White, Pamela. *The Psychology of Christian Nationalism: Why People are Drawn In and How to Talk Across the Divide*. Minneapolis: Fortress, 2022.

Corcoran, Katie E., et al. "Christian Nationalism and COVID-19 Vaccine Hesitancy and Uptake." *Vaccine* 39 (2021) 6614–21. https://www.ncbi.nlm.nih.gov/pmc/articles/PMC8489517/.

Craig, John. "Divorced Candidate Promotes Family Values." *The Spokesman Review*, July 31, 2008. https://www.spokesman.com/stories/2008/jul/31/divorced-candidate-promotes-family-values/.

Cramer, David, and Myles Werntz. *A Field Guide to Christian Nonviolence: Key Thinkers, Activists, and Movements for the Gospel of Peace*. Grand Rapids: Baker Academic, 2022.

Cramer, David C. "I Was a Christian Nationalist." *Anabaptist World*, August 18, 2023. https://anabaptistworld.org/i-was-a-christian-nationalist/.

Crenshaw, Kimberlé. "The Urgency of Intersectionality." December 7, 2016. https://www.youtube.com/watch?v=akOe5-UsQ2o.

Criscione, Wilson. "Spokane County Commission Candidate Rob Chase: 'I Didn't See Anything Wrong' with Rep. Shea's 'Biblical Basis for War.'"

Inlander, November 3, 2018. https://www.inlander.com/news/spokane-county-commission-candidate-rob-chase-i-didnt-see-anything-wrong-with-rep-sheas-biblical-basis-for-war-14086673.

Croasmun, Matthew. *The Emergence of Sin: The Cosmic Tyrant in Romans.* Oxford: Oxford University Press, 2017.

Davis, Jim, et al. *The Great Dechurching: Who's Leaving, Why Are They Going, and What Will It Take to Bring Them Back?* Grand Rapids: Zondervan, 2023.

"Deconstructing the Symbols and Slogans Spotted in Charlottesville." *Washington Post,* August 18, 2017. https://www.washingtonpost.com/graphics/2017/local/charlottesville-videos/.

DeCort, Andrew. "Christian Nationalism Is Tearing Ethiopia Apart." *Foreign Policy,* June 8, 2022. https://foreignpolicy.com/2022/06/18/ethiopia-pentecostal-evangelical-abiy-ahmed-christian-nationalism/.

Dehrone, Barsa M., et al. "Renewing American Democracy: Navigating a Changing Nation." Beyond Conflict, 2022. https://beyondconflictint.org/renewing-american-democracy.

DeMichele, Matthew, et al. "Research and Evaluation on Domestic Radicalization to Violent Extremism: Research to Support Exit USA." *National Criminal Justice Reference Service* (2021) 1–15. https://www.ojp.gov/pdffiles1/nij/grants/256037.pdf.

Dickinson, Tim. "He Has a 7-Point Plan for a Christian Takeover—and Wants Doug Mastriano to Lead the Charge." *Rolling Stone,* September 29, 2022. https://www.rollingstone.com/politics/politics-features/lance-wallnau-doug-mastriano-christian-dominion-1234602214/.

Draper, Andrew T. "The End of 'Mission': Christian Witness and the Decentering of White Identity." In *Can "White" People Be Saved? Triangulating Race, Theology, and Mission,* edited by Love L. Sechrest, et al., 177–205. Downers Grove, IL: IVP Academic, 2018.

Du Mez, Kristin Kobes. *Jesus and John Wayne: How White Evangelicals Corrupted a Faith and Fractured a Nation.* New York: Liveright, 2020.

Eklund, Rebekah. *Practicing Lament.* Eugene, OR: Cascade, 2021.

Ellsworth, Brian, and Fernando Cardoso. "Bolsonaro Shores Up Evangelical Support in Tight Brazil Election." *Reuters,* October 27, 2022. https://www.reuters.com/world/americas/bolsonaro-shores-up-evangelical-support-tight-brazil-election-2022-10-27/.

Fagan, Geraldine. "How the Russian Orthodox Church is Helping Drive Putin's War in Ukraine." *Time,* April 15, 2022. https://time.com/6167332/putin-russian-orthodox-church-war-ukraine/.

Flannery, Frances. "Radical Islamist and Radical Christianist Nuclear Terrorism." In *The Ecology of Violent Extremism: Perspectives on Peacebuilding and Human Security,* edited by Lisa Schirch, 81–86. New York: Rowman & Littlefield, 2018.

Florer-Bixler, Melissa. *How to Have an Enemy: Righteous Anger and the Work of Peace.* Harrisonburg, PA: Herald, 2021.

Frank, James. "Donald Rumsfeld's Bible Verses." *National Public Radio*, May 18, 2009. https://www.npr.org/sections/thetwo-way/2009/05/rumsfelds_bibleverse_briefings.html.

Fowl, Stephen E. *Idolatry*. Waco, TX: Baylor University Press, 2019.

Galtung, Johann. "Twenty-Five Years of Peace Research: Ten Challenges and Some Responses." *Journal of Peace Research* 22 (1985) 146–47.

Giridharadas, Anand. *The Persuaders: At the Front Lines of the Fight for Hearts, Minds, and Democracy*. New York: Alfred A. Knopf, 2022.

Goldberg, Michelle. *Kingdom Coming: The Rise of Christian Nationalism*. New York: W. W. Norton & Company, 2006.

González, Oriana. "D.C. Officer: 'It Was Clear the Terrorists Perceived Themselves to Be Christians.'" *Axios*, July 27, 2021. https://www.axios.com/2021/07/27/capitol-riot-terrorists-christians-police-attack.

Gorman, Michael J. *Inhabiting the Cruciform God: Kenosis, Justification, and Theosis in Paul's Narrative Soteriology*. Grand Rapids: Eerdmans, 2009.

———. *Reading Revelation Responsibly: Uncivil Worship and Witness Following the Lamb into the New Creation*. Eugene, OR: Cascade, 2011.

———. *Romans: A Theological and Pastoral Commentary*. Grand Rapids: Eerdmans, 2022.

Gorski, Philip. *American Covenant: A History of Civil Religion from the Puritans to the Present*. Princeton, NJ: Princeton University Press, 2017.

Gorski, Philip S., and Samuel L. Perry. *The Flag and the Cross: White Christian Nationalism and the Threat to American Democracy*. Oxford: Oxford University Press, 2022.

Graham, Franklin. "I was watching @60Minutes Sunday night & saw @LesleyRStahl's interview with @RepMTG. I learned a lot. I don't know her, but I think she brings some practical, common sense to politics. You might want to take a minute to check it out. It will be interesting to see how God uses her." Twitter, April 4, 2023, 9:21 a.m. https://twitter.com/franklin_graham/status/1643257491243802628?s=43&t=4QhQdpXbvSw8fu6A_e2XQg.

Gushee, David P. *Defending Democracy from Its Christian Enemies*. Grand Rapids: Eerdmans, 2023.

———. "My Argument in Defending Democracy." October 6, 2023. https://www.davidpgushee.com/my-argument-in-defending-democracy-from-its-christian-enemies/.

Hagen, Lisa. "The ReAwaken America Tour Unites Conservative Christians and Conspiracy Theorists." *National Public Radio*, November 3, 2022. https://www.npr.org/2022/11/02/1133477897/reawaken-america-brings-together-some-of-the-u-s-most-prolific-conspiracy-theori.

Halbertal, Moshe, and Avishai Margalit. *Idolatry*. Translated by Naomi Goldblum. Cambridge, MA: Harvard University Press, 1998.

Hauerwas, Stanley. *War and the American Difference: Theological Reflections on Violence and National Identity*. Grand Rapids: Baker Academic, 2011.

Hayden, Michael Edison. "'There's Nothing You Can Do': The Legacy of #Pizzagate." The Southern Poverty Law Center, July 7, 2021. https://www.splcenter.org/hatewatch/2021/07/07/theres-nothing-you-can-do-legacy-pizzagate.

Hays, Christopher B. "Isaiah as Colonized Poet: His Rhetoric of Death in Conversation with African Postcolonial Writers." In *Isaiah and Imperial Context: the Book of Isaiah in the Times of Empire*, edited by Andrew T. Abernethy, et al., 51–70. Eugene, OR: Pickwick, 2013.

Hsu, Spencer S. "Rage Met by Revulsion—First Jan. 6 Trial Shows Family, Nation Torn by Trump." *Washington Post,* March 4, 2022. https://www.washingtonpost.com/dc-md-va/2022/03/03/guy-reffitt-jan6-trial/.

Hummel, Daniel G. *The Rise and Fall of Dispensationalism: How the Evangelical Battle Over the End Times Shaped a Nation.* Grand Rapids: Eerdmans, 2023.

Inskeep, Steve. "Indiana Police Face Allegations of Police Brutality." *National Public Radio,* November 29, 2018. https://www.npr.org/2018/11/29/671799943/indiana-police-face-allegations-of-police-brutality.

Jeffress, Robert. *The Gift: The Gospel for Children.* Dallas: Pathway to Victory, 2017.

Jennings, Willie James. *Acts: A Theological Commentary on the Bible.* Louisville, KY: Westminster John Knox, 2017.

———. "To Be a Christian Intellectual." Yale Divinity School, October 30, 2015. https://divinity.yale.edu/news/willie-jennings-be-christian-intellectual.

Jones, Robert P. "A Virtual Roundtable on the Threat of Christian Nationalism, Part 1 of 4 by Robert P. Jones." White Too Long, February 9, 2023. https://robertpjones.substack.com/p/a-virtual-roundtable-on-the-threat.

Keddie, Tony. *Republican Jesus: How the Right Has Rewritten the Gospels.* Oakland, CA: University of California Press, 2020.

Kleinfeld, Rachel. "The Rise in Political Violence in the United States and Damage to Our Democracy." Carnegie Endowment for International Peace, March 31, 2022. https://carnegieendowment.org/2022/03/31/rise-in-political-violence-in-united-states-and-damage-to-our-democracy-pub-87584.

Kotsko, Adam. *Neoliberalism's Demons: On the Political Theology of Late Capital.* Stanford: Stanford University Press, 2018.

Ladner, Keri. "The Quiet Rise of Christian Dominionism." *The Christian Century,* November, 2022. https://www.christiancentury.org/article/features/quiet-rise-christian-dominionism.

Leary, John Patrick. "What is Neoliberalism? An Economic and Political System Devoted to the Free Market." *Teen Vogue,* March 14, 2023. https://www.teenvogue.com/story/what-is-neoliberalism.

Lederach, John Paul. *Building Peace: Sustainable Reconciliation in Divided Societies.* Washington, DC: United States Institute of Peace, 1997.

————. *Conflict Transformation: Clear Articulation of the Guiding Principles by a Pioneer in the Field.* New York: Good, 2003.

Levine, Amy-Jill. "Alumni Profiles." Duke Graduate School, November 17, 2021. https://gradschool.duke.edu/professional-development/blog/alumni-profiles-series-amy-jill-levine/.

Lopez, Brian. "Texas Public Schools Required to Display 'In God We Trust' Poster if They Are Donated." *The Texas Tribune*, August 18, 2022. https://www.texastribune.org/2022/08/18/texas-schools-in-god-we-trust/.

Marron, Dylan. *Conversations with People Who Hate Me: 12 Things I Learned from Talking to Internet Strangers.* New York: Atria, 2022.

————. "Empathy is Not Endorsement." May 18, 2018. https://www.youtube.com/watch?v=waVUm5bhLbg&t=35s.

Marzurek, Marek. "Elkhart Officials, Business Leaders Propose Development Plans for Benham West Area." *WVPE News*, August 15, 2023. https://www.wvpe.org/wvpe-news/2023-08-15/elkhart-officials-business-leaders-propose-development-plans-for-benham-west-area.

Mascia, Jennifer, and Chip Brownlee. "How Many Guns are Circulating in the U.S.?" *The Trace*, March 6, 2023. https://www.thetrace.org/2023/03/guns-america-data-atf-total/.

McDonald, Cassidy. "Man Who Swung from Senate Balcony on January 6 Pleads Guilty and Agrees to Cooperate." *CBS News*, July 14, 2021. https://www.cbsnews.com/news/january-6-capitol-riot-josiah-colt-senate-chamber-guilty-plea/.

McKnight, Scot. *The Bible Is Not Enough: Imagination and Making Peace in the Modern World.* Minneapolis: Fortress, 2023.

————. *The King Jesus Gospel: The Original Good News Revisited.* Grand Rapids: Zondervan, 2011.

Miller, Paul D. *The Religion of American Greatness: What's Wrong with Christian Nationalism.* Downers Grove, IL: IVP Academic, 2022.

Mogelson, Luke. "A Reporter's Video from Inside the Capitol Siege. The New Yorker." January 6, 2021. https://www.newyorker.com/video/watch/a-reporters-footage-from-inside-the-capitol-siege.

Moonshot. "Mental Health and Violent Extremism." https://moonshotteam.com/wp-content/uploads/Moonshot-CVE-Mental-Health-and-Violent-Extremism.pdf.

————. "The Redirect Method." https://moonshotteam.com/the-redirect-method/.

————. "Time Impact of COVID-19 on Canadian Search Traffic." June 2020. https://149736141.v2.pressablecdn.com/wp-content/uploads/The-Impact-of-COVID-19-on-Canadian-Search-Traffic_Moonshot-CVE.pdf.

Mutz, Diana. "Status Threat, Not Economic Hardship, Explain the 2016 Presidential Vote." *Proceedings of the National Academy of Sciences* 115 (2018).

National Immigration Forum. "The 'Great Replacement' Theory, Explained." https://immigrationforum.org/wp-content/uploads/2021/12/Replacement-Theory-Explainer-1122.pdf.

Newsom, Carol A. "God's Other: The Intractable Problem of the Gentile King in Judean and Early Jewish Literature." In *The Other in Second Temple Judaism: Essays in Honor of John J. Collins*, edited by Daniel C. Harlow, et al., 31–48. Grand Rapids: Eerdmans, 2011.

Noll, Mark A., et al. *The Search for Christian America*. Westchester, IL: Crossway, 1983.

O'Harrow, Robert, Jr., et al. "The Rise of Domestic Extremism in America." *The Washington Post*, April 12, 2021. https://www.washingtonpost.com/investigations/interactive/2021/domestic-terrorism-data/.

Onishi, Bradley. *Preparing for War: The Extremist History of White Christian Nationalism—and What Comes Next*. Minneapolis: Broadleaf, 2023.

Osmundsen, Mathias, et al. "Partisan Polarization is the Primary Psychological Motivation Behind Political Fake News Sharing on Twitter." *American Political Science Review* 115 (2021) 999–1015. https://www.cambridge.org/core/journals/american-political-science-review/article/abs/partisan-polarization-is-the-primary-psychological-motivation-behind-political-fake-news-sharing-on-twitter/3F7D2098CD87AE5501F7AD4A7FA83602.

"Our Epidemic of Loneliness and Isolation." 2023. https://www.hhs.gov/sites/default/files/surgeon-general-social-connection-advisory.pdf.

Parker, Angela. *If God Still Breathes, Why Can't I? Black Lives Matter and Biblical Authority*. Grand Rapids: Eerdmans, 2021.

Pasternack, Alex. "One Secret Weapon against Extremism: Google Ads Promoting Mindfulness." Fast Company, March 11, 2021. https://www.fastcompany.com/90607977/moonshot-digital-counter-radicalization-google-ads-mindfulness-redirect-method.

"The Persistence of QAnon in the Post-Trump Era: An Analysis of Who Believes the Conspiraces." Public Religion Research Institute, February 24, 2022. https://www.prri.org/research/the-persistence-of-qanon-in-the-post-trump-era-an-analysis-of-who-believes-the-conspiracies/.

"Pillars of Power." https://beautifultrouble.org/toolbox/tool/pillars-of-power/.

Portier-Young, Anathea. "Apocalyptic Preaching." Working Preacher, June 1, 2009. https://www.workingpreacher.org/theology-and-interpretation/apocalyptic-preaching.

Posner, Sarah. *Unholy: How White Christian Nationalists Powered the Trump Presidency, and the Devastating Legacy They Left Behind*. New York: Random House, 2021.

Rago, Gordon. "In God We Trust Decals Will Go on All Chesapeake City Vehicles." *The Virginian-Pilot*, July 14, 2021. https://www.pilotonline.com/2021/07/14/in-god-we-trust-decals-will-go-on-all-chesapeake-city-vehicles/.

Reed, Brad. "Pastor Alarmed after Trump-Loving Congregants Deride Jesus' Teachings as 'Weak.'" RawStory, August 9, 2023. https://www.rawstory.com/trump-evangelicals-2663078391/.

Rogers-Vaughn, Bruce. *Caring for Souls in a Neoliberal Age.* New York: Palgrave Macmillan, 2016.

Schiess, Kaitlyn. *The Bible and the Ballot: How Scripture Has Been Used and Abused in American Politics and Where We Go From Here.* Grand Rapids: Brazos, 2023.

Schirch, Lisa. *The Little Book of Strategic Peacebuilding: A Vision and Framework for Peace with Justice.* New York: Good, 2004.

———. "Making Peace in a Violent World." MennoMedia. https://dhjhkxawhe8q4.cloudfront.net/mennomedia-wp/wp-content/uploads/2021/10/11205333/What-Now-October-2021-Navigating-polarization-Making-Peace-in-a-Violent-World.pdf.

———. "Mapping the Ecology of Violent Extremism: Correlations and Theories of Change." In *The Ecology of Violent Extremism: Perspectives on Peacebuilding and Human Security,* edited by Lisa Schirch, 21–52. New York: Rowman & Littlefield, 2018.

———. *Social Media Impacts on Conflict and Democracy: The Techtonic Shift,* edited by Lisa Schirch. New York: Routledge, 2021.

———. "Transforming the Colour of US Peacebuilding: Types of Dialogue to Protect and Advance Multi-Racial Democracy." *Toda Peace Institute Policy Brief* 114 (2021) 1–17.

Schirch, Lisa, and David Campt. *The Little Book of Dialogue for Difficult Subjects: A Practical, Hands-On Guide.* Intercourse, PA: Good Books, 2015.

Seibert, Eric. *Disarming the Church.* Eugene, OR: Cascade, 2018.

Seidel, Andrew L. *The Founding Myth: Why Christian Nationalism is Un-American.* New York: Sterling, 2021.

Sharlet, Jeff. *The Undertow: Scenes from a Slow Civil War.* New York: W. W. Norton, 2023.

Sharp, Gene. *The Politics of Nonviolent Action.* Boston: Porter Sargent, 1973.

———. *Sharp's Dictionary of Power and Struggle: Language of Civil Resistance.* Oxford: Oxford University Press, 2012.

———. *Waging Nonviolent Struggle: 20th Century Practice and 21st Century Potential.* Boston: Extending Horizon Books, 2005.

Slachmuijlder, Lena. "Peacebuilding Narratives and Countering Violent Extremism." In *The Ecology of Violence Extremism: Perspectives on Peacebuilding and Human Security,* edited by Lisa Schirch, 284–90. New York: Rowman & Littlefield, 2018.

Smith, Christian. *The Bible Made Impossible: Why Biblicism Is Not a Truly Evangelical Reading of Scripture.* Grand Rapids: Brazos, 2011.

Smith, Gregory A., et al. "45% of Americans Say U.S. Should Be a 'Christian Nation.'" Pew Research Center, October 27, 2022. https://www.pewresearch.org/religion/2022/10/27/45-of-americans-say-u-s-should-be-a-christian-nation/.

———. "Views of the U.S. as a 'Christian Nation' and Opinions About 'Christian Nationalism.'" Pew Research Center, October 27, 2022. https://www.pewresearch.org/religion/2022/10/27/views-of-the-u-s-as-a-christian-nation-and-opinions-about-christian-nationalism/.

Smucker, Jonathan Matthew. *Hegemony How-To: A Roadmap for Radicals.* Baltimore: AK, 2017.

"Spectrum of Allies." Beautiful Trouble. https://beautifultrouble.org/toolbox/tool/spectrum-of-allies/

"START, National Consortium for the Study of Terrorism and Responses to Terrorism." University of Maryland, 2021. https://www.start.umd.edu/sites/default/files/publications/local_attachments/START%20QAnon%20Research%20Brief_24September2021.pdf.

Steger, Manfred B., and Ravi K. Roy. *Neoliberalism: A Very Short Introduction.* Oxford: Oxford University Press, 2021.

Steinmetz-Jenkins, Daniel. "Christianity's Place in the Left and the Right." *The Nation*, March 29, 2023. https://www.thenation.com/article/society/qa-david-hollinger-religous-right/.

Stewart, Emily. "Sarah Sanders on Immigrant Family Separation: 'It is Very Biblical to Enforce the Law.'" *Vox*, June 14, 2018. https://www.vox.com/2018/6/14/17465662/sarah-sanders-family-separation-bible-sessions.

Strait, Drew J. "Christian Nationalism's Superstition Problem." Political Theology Network, October 16, 2023. https://politicaltheology.com/christian-nationalisms-superstition-problem/.

———. *Hidden Criticism of the Angry Tyrant in Early Judaism and the Acts of the Apostles.* New York: Lexington/Fortress Academic, 2019.

———. "Idols, Idolatry." In *The Dictionary of Paul and His Letters: A Compendium of Contemporary Biblical Scholarship*, edited by Scot McKnight, et al., 467–69. Downers Grove, IL: IVP Academic, 2023.

———. "Let's Talk about 'Christian Nationalism.'" *Christianity Today*, August 26, 2020. https://www.christianitytoday.com/scot-mcknight/2020/august/lets-talk-about-christian-nationalism.html.

———. "The Myth of Redemptive Violence." Made for Pax. https://www.madeforpax.org/nonviolence/myth.

———. "A Pastoral Approach to Resisting Christian Nationalism's Influence in the Local Congregation." *Brethren in Christ History and Life* 46 (2023) 57–81.

———. "Political Idolatry and White Christian Nationalism: Toward a Pastoral Hermeneutic of Resistance." *Mennonite Quarterly Review* 96 (2022) 47–72.

———. "What is Christian Nationalism and Why is It a Problem?" *Brethren in Christ History and Life* 46 (2023) 37–56.

Stroop, Chrissy. "Christian Nationalism is Authentically Christian—And According to a New Poll Most White Evangelicals are Supporters." *Religion Dispatches*, February 9, 2023. https://religiondispatches.org/christian-nationalism-is-authentically-christian-and-according-to-a-new-poll-most-white-evangelicals-are-supporters/.

Suliman, Adela, and Timothy Bella. "GOP Rep. Boebert: 'I'm Tired of This Separation of Church and State Junk.'" *The Washington Post*, June 28, 2022. https://www.washingtonpost.com/politics/2022/06/28/lauren-boebert-church-state-colorado/.

Taylor, David. "'In God We Trust'—The Bills Christian Nationalists Hope Will 'Protect Religious Freedom.'" *The Guardian*, January 14, 2019. https://www.theguardian.com/us-news/2019/jan/14/christian-nationalists-bills-religious-freedom-project-blitz.

Taylor, Matthew. "Charismatic Revival Fury." *Straight White American Jesus Podcast.* https://www.straightwhiteamericanjesus.com/series/charismatic-revival-fury/.

———. "Charismatic Revival Fury, Ep2: Modern-Day Apostles and the Spiritual Oligarchy." *Straight White American Jesus Podcast,* December 12, 2022. https://www.straightwhiteamericanjesus.com/episodes/charismatic-revival-fury-ep-2-modern-day-apostles-and-the-spiritual-oligarchy/.

"Threats to American Democracy Ahead of an Unprecedented Presidential Election." Public Religion Research Institute, October 25, 2023. https://www.prri.org/research/threats-to-american-democracy-ahead-of-an-unprecedented-presidential-election/.

Tisby, Jemar. "Engaging White Christian Nationalism in Public Spaces." August 18, 2021. https://raac.iupui.edu/programs/events/White-christian-nationalism-in-the-united-states-an-online-mini-conference/.

———. "A Virtual Roundtable on the Threat of Christian Nationalism, Part 2 of 4 by Jemar Tisby." Footnotes by Jemar Tisby, February 12, 2023. https://jemartisby.substack.com/p/a-virtual-roundtable-on-the-threat?utm_source=substack&utm_campaign=post_embed&utm_medium=web.

Torba, Andrew, and Andrew Isker. *Christian Nationalism: A Biblical Guide to Taking Dominion and Discipling Nations.* Self-published: GAB AI Inc., 2022.

"U.S. Military Weapons Inscribed With Secret 'Jesus' Bible Codes." *ABC News*, January 15, 2010. https://abcnews.go.com/Blotter/us-military-weapons-inscribed-secret-jesus-bible-codes/story?id=9575794.

Villagran, Lauren. "Walmart Shooter Allegedly Penned White Supremacist Rant in 'Bible of Evil.'" *El Paso Times*, August 4, 2019. https://www.elpasotimes.com/story/news/2019/08/04/el-paso-shooting-patrick-crusius-white-supremacist-manifesto/1914965001/.

Volf, Miroslav. *Public Faith: How Followers of Christ Should Serve the Common Good.* Grand Rapids: Brazos, 2011.

———. "The Social Meaning of Reconciliation." *Interpretation* 54 (2000) 158–72.

Vosoughi, Soroush, et al. "The Spread of True and False News Online." *Science* 359 (2018) 1146–51.

Walker, Brooklyn, and Abigail Vegter. "Christ, Country, and Conspiracies? Christian Nationalism, Biblical Literalism, and Belief in Conspiracy Theories." *Journal for the Scientific Study of Religion* 62 (2023) 1–15.

Washington, James M., ed. *I Have a Dream: Writings and Speeches That Changed the World.* New York: Harper One, 1986.

Weinfeld, Moshe. "The Protest against Imperialism in Ancient Israelite Prophecy." In *The Origins and Diversity of Axial Age Civilizations*, edited by S. N. Eisenstadt, 169–82. Albany: State University of New York Press, 1986.

Wengst, Klaus. *Pax Romana and the Peace of Jesus Christ.* Translated by John Bowden. Munich: SCM, 1987.

Wermund, Benjamin. "Exclusive: Texas Troopers Told to Push Children into Rio Grande, Deny Water to Migrants, Records Say." *Houston Chronicle*, July 21, 2023. https://www.houstonchronicle.com/politics/texas/article/border-trooper-migrants-wire-18205076.php.

Whitaker, Robyn. *Even the Devil Quotes Scripture: Reading the Bible on its Own Terms.* Grand Rapids: Eerdmans, 2023.

Whitehead, Andrew L. *American Idolatry: How Christian Nationalism Threatens the Gospel and Betrays the Church.* Grand Rapids: Brazos, 2023.

Whitehead, Andrew L. and Samuel L. Perry, *Taking America Back for God: Christian Nationalism in the United States.* Oxford: Oxford University Press, 2020.

"Why Do Our Brains Love Fake News?" PBS Learning Media. https://illinois.pbslearningmedia.org/resource/bias-brain-kqed/why-do-our-brains-love-fake-news-above-the-noise/.

Wilkerson, Isabel. *Caste: The Origins of Our Discontents.* New York: Random House, 2020.

Williams, Daniel K. "What Really Happens When Americans Stop Going to Church." *The Atlantic*, September 3, 2023. https://www.theatlantic.com/ideas/archive/2023/09/christianity-religion-america-church-polarization/675215/?taid=64f9868b25b31200017b1d03&utm_campaign=theatlantic&utm_content=true-anthem&utm_medium=social&utm_source=twitter.

Wilson, Rainn. "The metamorphosis of Jesus Christ from a humble servant of the abject poor to a symbol that stands for gun rights, prosperity theology, anti-science, limited government (that neglects the destitute) and fierce nationalism is truly the strangest transformation in human history." Twitter, August 3, 2029, 2:35 PM. https://twitter.com/rainnwilson/status/1157736650274828288?lang=en.

Yoder, Perry. *Shalom: The Bible's Word for Salvation, Justice, and Peace.* Eugene, OR: Wipf & Stock, 2017.

Yoder-Short, Jane. "Opinion: So, Just What Would a Christian Nation Look Like?" *Yahoo News*, May 6, 2023. https://news.yahoo.com/opinion-just-christian-nation-look-150709384.html?guccounter=1.

Zaimov, Stoyan. "Donald Trump: 'Nobody Reads Bible More Than Me: John Kerry Hasn't Read the Bible.'" *Christian Post*, February 25, 2016. https://www.christianpost.com/news/donald-trump-nobody-reads-bible-more-than-me-john-kerry.html.

Zauzumer, Julie, and Keith McMillan. "Sessions Cites Bible Passage Used to Defend Slavery in Defense of Separating Immigrant Families." June 15, 2018. https://www.washingtonpost.com/news/acts-of-faith/wp/2018/06/14/jeff-sessions-points-to-the-bible-in-defense-of-separating-immigrant-families/.

Printed in Great Britain
by Amazon

62509611R00102